Praise for

The Adversity Hack

"Make life deeper and more joyful! Meg has a natural way of explaining things, offering good, relevant examples, and showing us a clear-cut method to developing our spiritual intelligence (SQ). SQ changes how we see things, giving us much better options for living life with wisdom and compassion. Use *The Adversity Hack* to break out of old habits and find sustainable joy."

—**CINDY WIGGLESWORTH,** MA, best-selling author of *SQ21: The Twenty-One Skills of Spiritual Intelligence* and Founder and President of Deep Change, Inc.

"I recommend Meg's excellent guidelines to anyone wanting to turn stress into sound action."

—**DR. BARRY MORGUELAN,** Founder of Energy for Success, world-renowned surgeon, and pioneer in gastroenterology

The Adversity Hack

Get Out of Your Own Way,
Shift Your Thinking, and
Change Your World

Meg Poag

RIVER GROVE
BOOKS

Published by River Grove Books
Austin, TX
www.rivergrovebooks.com

Distributed by River Grove Books

Design and composition by Greenleaf Book Group and Lindsay Starr
Cover design by Greenleaf Book Group and Lindsay Starr

Publisher's Cataloging-in-Publication data is available.

Print ISBN: 978-1-63299-419-6

eBook ISBN: 978-1-63299-420-2

First Edition

This book is dedicated to all my clients who diligently explored this crazy work with me and opened themselves up to this powerful tool. Your vulnerability, honesty, courage, and growth inspired me to create this book. Thank you for honoring me with your trust and engagement in this work!

"I'm trying to free your mind, Neo. But I can only show you the door. You're the one that has to walk through it."

—MORPHEUS, THE MATRIX

CONTENTS

PREFACE

We've all seen inspiring quotes like "Things always turn out for the best," and "Everything you want is on the other side of fear." OK, these are nice sentiments. When I read this kind of wisdom, I'm reflective for about 2.5 seconds. Then I turn back to my same old life, live by my same old patterns, and experience the same frustrations, anger, hurt, resentments, and regrets about my past choices, big or small. And I would appreciate those small moments of joy, surprise, or having things to look forward to, but they were just a moment or two per day, with a lot of doldrums and frustrations in between.

For the longest time, I thought this was just the nature of existence. While I accepted it, I hated those intense moments of sadness, regret, resentment, and anger toward the people around me, politicians I read about in the news, or pretty much anyone or anything I blamed for making me unhappy or undermining my efforts.

I experienced these moments over and over. And I accepted this dull, depressing reality because it was largely accepted by those around me, particularly when it came to work. We spend so much time at work, allowing our jobs to suck our passion and inspiration right out of us. So many of us passively float along in our professional tracks and our daily work experience. And most of us just accept that work kind of sucks and that it's generally not going to be fulfilling, and we'll probably never have that "dream job," since it only exists for that rare sliver of the working population that's incredibly talented and driven, or super lucky.

But I, like many people, eventually hit a point when it was all too much for me to bear, and I sought help. I found a therapist, an executive coach, a loving friend, a spiritual guide, and a mentor. I'd ask them to tell me how to get out of my pain and maybe even how to get what I wanted in life. For a short while I'd feel uplifted and guided to make different choices, and then, for a brief moment of clarity, I'd see the fruits of those choices in my life! But then, in all my brilliant humanity, I'd walk away from the support and guidance that I was given and completely regress.

This, of course, resulted in my experiencing the same old frustrations and resentments. I still had the same lame workday that left me exhausted and lifeless. I still had the same frustrations of not feeling valued at work, not knowing if I was really making the difference I wanted to make. And I still had the same enraging situations and feelings of being stuck, undervalued, and overwhelmed.

And then I started to reflect on this cycle. I began to wonder if it was simply the nature of human existence to suffer over and over. Were my dreams of feeling peaceful, loved, supported, accepted, powerful, successful, and joyful all a joke? Was it all some giant trick? Was my dream of having fulfilling, thrilling work an impossibility? And was it completely unrealistic of me to want to work with people who loved their jobs and showed up with their whole selves to create something awesome together?

After careful consideration I came to an astounding conclusion: Hell no! I do *not* have to accept this as my fate. And you don't either!

It seems everyone has different advice for how to emerge from suffering and experience more joy, based largely on how they have worked through the suffering and come out the other side. Unfortunately, much of their advice might not quite work for you. There are thousands of people—authors, professionals, perhaps even some friends—who want to help you and have tried to no avail. All the books, advice, coaching—it can become overwhelming. It also might not be what you're looking for, and it might not *work*. And maybe you're not sure what you want or what kind of a life is even possible for you. Sound familiar?

Well, I'm going to tell you something that may surprise you: You have everything you need to do this yourself. And you've already got a ton of talents, strengths, and experiences to apply to this effort. What if all you needed was a simple but powerful tool to get on a path that actually works? What if there were a tool that took all that age-old wisdom and priceless guidance, and enabled you to apply it to *your* life—to change your life by changing the way you were thinking and living—so you could recreate the world around you?

Sounds too good to be true, right? Well, I've been using the Adversity Cycle with hundreds of people—tailoring it and perfecting it—and I have never seen it fail when someone is committed to using it. In fact, I've devoted most of my professional life to helping leaders in the workplace find their joy, so they can interact with more empathy, rapidly tap into their superpowers, identify their blind spots, and leap over the hurdles that have stifled them for years.

This book will help you dramatically improve your emotional intelligence. It will help you transcend the things you struggle with now so you will not have to struggle with them in the future. You also will realize what you want and discover what brings you joy. You will know exactly how you want to live and what you need to do to get there.

This one tool changed my thinking profoundly. It altered my feelings, my experience of everyday circumstances, and eventually the world around me. But first I had to take the hardest step anyone takes on this journey: I had to confront the undeniable truth that it was all me. All the pain, suffering, mistakes, lost hopes, lost dreams—I'd done this to myself. And I had no idea how or why. But finally there was nothing and no one else to blame. And that's when my real journey began.

—MEG POAG
Austin, Texas
April 2021

Introduction

Welcome to the Journey!

Clearly, you care about your life and your happiness enough to pick up this book and do some work. That's thrilling! No journey in my life has been as rewarding as this one, and I want to share it in a way that will work for you, so your results will be powerful, fast, efficient, and mind-blowingly transformative. This will be the most rewarding journey you ever take.

This book is my gift to you. It is my hope that it serves you on your journey as it has for me, my clients, my friends, and my family. By experimenting with the different approaches in this book and learning more about yourself and what you want in life, you will experience the inevitable ripple effect from your new choices, beliefs, and behaviors—quickly and powerfully.

The Problem

Simply stated, the problem is this: We believe we're stuck in a state of intermittent frustration, pain, resentment, and suffering. But guess what? That's all a lie that has been programmed into almost all of us since day one.

I found myself at a point in my life where I felt I should feel happy. I had, with luck and hard work, achieved so much that I had thought would make me happy, and there I was, more miserable than ever. There was nothing wrong with me diagnostically. I had had a fairly normal and blessed life in so many ways. I had a great husband, an awesome little kiddo, and a safe and comfortable home. I also lived in a cool city, was surrounded by great friends, and had an executive job doing meaningful work. But each day it was a struggle to *want* to live my life. I numbed myself from disappointment and anger by pretending it wasn't there or indulging in an almost nightly glass of wine. I had pangs of resentment and frustration hundreds of times a day. I was, like so many others, searching for that one thing that would make me happy. But because I was placing responsibility for my joy outside of myself, happiness and joy evaded me.

I had all kinds of useless beliefs that I had been programmed to believe, such as "you have to work your ass off to have any chance at financial stability in this world." I never thought to question these beliefs that sucked the joy out of my life and obscured millions of beautiful opportunities from my view. It was the worst trick life could play on me, and I fell for it—hook, line, and sinker. And I had no idea where to go.

So, I finally sucked it up and said "enough" and started down a path that would turn out to be a journey of immense struggle, confusion, pain, and—strange as it might seem—humor and boundless hope. I've taken the best discoveries and tools that have worked for me and my clients and shaped them into a self-coaching tool to guide you along the way.

This tool has transformed me and, by association, the world around me. I took an earnest look at how hard I was working every day as well as how frustrated I was all day and thought, *Is this really what you want, Meg? Is something else possible? Why are you even doing this?*

Those questions, sparked by the tool in this book, caused me to own up to how I was spending my time. In turn, I set different priorities that would bring me more joy and fulfillment. I began to see all the opportunities for, and find the time for, fun and connection with the people I most wanted to spend time with. My husband and son got to experience me smiling and playing with them way more. And because of that we were all transformed.

Since then, over the last several years I've used this tool with hundreds of individuals in my work as an organizational development consultant and leadership coach and have refined and tested it like crazy. I've witnessed the magic of people using it and waking up just like I did. It brought me such joy when they realized they had everything they needed to change their world and overcome all the bullshit patterns in their lives so they could realize their dreams. Suddenly they felt they could do things they previously thought were impossible. They stood bravely in the face of their fears and the lies they believed, and they laughed and cried their way to being forever changed.

What This Book Isn't

There's already a bunch of thinking and writing out there about waking up, emotional intelligence, enlightenment, psychology, and how to approach your life more effectively. There are lots of collections of thought (books, articles, podcasts, blogs, etc.) that are just that—collections of ideas, facts, and even some strategies. But it's time for a tool that's actually usable and effective.

This isn't a deep, comprehensive study. This book does not contain hollow inspiration or any deep-dives into the obtuse. It isn't a thorough study of any one subject area, but rather a pragmatic summary and application of key lessons that are consistent across multiple disciplines, including neuroscience, behavioral psychology, and various paths to enlightenment. This book offers an applied technology in human growth and transformation for you to use, or not—your choice. I've read a lot, studied a lot, meditated a lot, and helped other people use this tool *a lot*. I've tested the concepts and process with my clients and formed a relatively simple, clear tool for anyone to use.

I know that you are already fully capable of using a tool to change your life fundamentally and forever. That said, this is, in many respects, a "how-to" book as opposed to a "what if" book. There are likely volumes of books covering in detail the concepts on any given page of this book. This is an overview of the most important considerations for you to actually *use* to change your life, without too much naval-gazing.

This isn't a book on how to be happy or how to take control of your life. Happiness is an emotion, not a state of being. And control is an illusion. This is about a set of skills and muscles you can build to live your dreams and shift your inner world. You cannot control the outer world completely, but you can control your experience of it and influence what you can, and thus increase your volition in the world around you. (You know, just that tiny mission of making your dreams a reality.)

So, instead of making happiness your goal, reach for joy. Happiness comes from events occurring outside of you in your environment. Joy comes from the inside—from your efforts to live in ways that create fulfillment, peace, and vibrant gratitude for your life. You cannot control everything around you. But you can change the way you interact with the world and influence it in intentional, positive ways. Stop trying to control everything to grab at more happiness. Get intentional about your influence instead. In this work, we make joy our North Star, not happiness.

This book isn't intended to be a therapeutic tool or self-help manual. Traditional self-help offers advice on how to improve your life. I am not an expert telling you what to think or do, or not think or not do. I believe that only you know you. You know what you want, and ultimately only you can see what's actually holding you back. This book is here to help you identify and unbelieve the lies that are holding you back so you can wake up to your true nature and know what brings you joy and exactly how to fight for it and win. Rather than providing advice, this book offers you a tool you can use to rebuild your life.

What This Book IS

Simply put, this is a guidebook for walking a new kind path through your life. You can also think of it as a kind of life hack. A life hack is defined as a clever tip or technique for accomplishing some familiar task more easily and efficiently. In this case, I present to you an instructional manual to hack your approach to how you live your life. And it's all built on how you approach adversity. Yep, it's that simple!

Instead of letting adversity and challenges trick you and knock you sideways, you can actually use them as your number one source of learning and strength as you improve your life. This guidebook will walk you through the Adversity Cycle, a path that will help you become your own therapist, coach, advisor, mentor, Sherpa, and guide. The Adversity Cycle allows you to hack adversity (that stuff you tend to hate and resent) so you can wake up to what's holding you back and transform your life. You might just become addicted to adversity, like me, because when you experience it, you know that you're about to learn something invaluable. I'm a pragmatist, and I truly believe that if I can do this, anyone can. I'm not remotely unique, nor are the many clients I've worked with who have transformed their lives by choosing this path.

How to Use This Book

Be open and ready to unlearn some lies you currently believe. You've been fooled into believing a bunch of things that don't serve you, don't work, and aren't in accordance with physics and the way things actually work. The Adversity Cycle will reveal these tricks and help you prove their fallibility. Inner peace is not just for monks, and abundance is not just for the rich. You don't have to shelter yourself away from the world and meditate for ten hours a day to have inner peace, harmony, and joy. And conversely, you don't have to be greedy or self-obsessed to realize a life of abundance. Be open to examining those thoughts that have been in the back of your mind for as long as you can remember and ask yourself if they are, in fact, true or helpful.

The Adversity Cycle pulls together proven principles and research-based strategies from an array of disciplines. These principles will test your existing assumptions and beliefs about life. They will challenge the way you currently think. And that's a good thing! If you keep believing the same things, you'll keep behaving in the same ways and getting the same results, right?

The teachings in this book have been tested over and over with a ton of people and are based largely on my own journey *and* my journey of helping others do this work. I've refined the tool based on what I discovered during my coaching experience to make it as effective and efficient as possible. This book is a body of work and ideas that stands on the shoulders of intellectual and spiritual giants. I've taken some powerful teachings from super smart, revolutionary thinkers and collected them into an organized path for you to navigate, but we are all standing on their shoulders, so I want to be sure to acknowledge that here. The ideas in this book are not new or unique! They are pulled from numerous texts, research, and teachings in emotional intelligence, neuroscience, social/ behavioral psychology, spirituality, and existentialism. I've also included a Resources section at the back of the book, so you can do some more reading and thinking as you become curious and want to discover more.

Roll up your sleeves. This is all about improving your abilities (skills, beliefs, behaviors, and attributes) that will lead to a life of joy and fulfillment. It's the hardest work you may ever do but by far the most rewarding. It's not time-consuming or earth-shattering. It's basic, but it requires the discipline, curiosity, and humility to build new muscle.

The Adversity Cycle infuses and builds on concepts of what some people call emotional intelligence and others refer to as existential or spiritual intelligence. Different definitions exist for emotional intelligence, so to clarify, I'm taking the definition of the skills involved in emotional intelligence to their broadest sense. Essentially, it's identifying emotion accurately, learning how to function at a higher level, and navigating relationships judiciously and empathetically. Whereas existential or spiritual intelligence extends emotional intelligence skills into the realm of learning who you are, what you're meant to do and be, how the universe works, and how to align yourself with it. Sounds like some useful skills to develop, right? And yes, you've already figured out much of this and developed a lot of skills in these realms.

Here's the interesting dynamic: Your negative responses to adversity present you with the exact areas of skill and awareness you have yet to develop. Your upset or negative emotions point you toward the areas of your life where you require some learning and growth. So get ready to level up, my friends!

Please note: This tool is not religious, theological, or supportive of any particular belief system. It's a path to knowing yourself and figuring out your beliefs and your place in the world. I have found that our modern, mainstream culture has turned away from important lessons in emotional and social well-being. We also seem to not place a lot of value on learning how to live a life of meaning, or the teachings that have historically been left to existential and spiritual texts and disciplines. These lessons don't need to be pedantic, strident, rigid, or judgmental. Yet many of us have had experiences, especially with religion, that have turned us away from exploring greater truths and meaning in our lives. This book brings you back to these explorations to find out who you really are. In the process you will uncover what you really want, who you want to be, and how you want to move through your life. This awareness allows you to transform your experience of life to realize those things.

If you're experiencing strife, struggle, or suffering, you have work to do. If you're not sure what your purpose is in life, you have work to do. If you haven't experienced deep, lasting fulfillment, you have work to do. This is your book!

*But don't take my word for it. **TRY IT OUT***. Please don't believe anything I say just because you're reading it! Question it, struggle with it, and, most importantly, test it out for yourself. See if it serves you. Judge the path I've laid out by what it brings to your life. This body of thought creates a platform for experimentation and exploration. Use it as a treasure map for your life.

This book will show you how to glide through challenges in life. The things that used to stress you out or that you thought were so hard will soon seem inconsequential. Usually it takes us a lot of trial and error and a lot of time to work through things. I wanted to find a way to accelerate that learning dramatically. To my knowledge, the Adversity Cycle is the only self-guided, comprehensive tool to increase your emotional intelligence, efficacy, and success in any aspect of your life. When using the tool, you'll make better decisions, get less upset by things, and experience more joy and less suffering. All from one little process of personal transformation.

*Sound too good to be true? **IT'S NOT***. Many people throughout history have gotten there. But they often weren't sure how they did or how to help others. In this book, I've created a proven path that anyone can follow to achieve growth and transformation at an incredibly rapid rate. So engage in the steps and activities. Apply them to your life and your struggles. Explore the path and take some time to reflect. Is it working?

What are you uncovering? Has it been helpful? In what ways? You don't need to believe any of it. Just play with it and make it yours!

How This Book Is Set Up

I've structured this book in a way that will allow you to navigate your growth process in a simple and enjoyable way. It is divided into three parts:

Part 1: The Desire for Transformation

Part 2: The Adversity Cycle

Part 3: Living the Adversity Cycle

Part 1 dives right into the nature of this tool and the work you will do as you progress on the path of personal transformation. It also covers what you will come up against and how the tool can support you through those challenges. Finally, it jumps right into the foundational skills you'll need to use the 4-Step Adversity Cycle, as well as how to master them.

Part 2 walks you through the Adversity Cycle tool itself. You'll learn how to approach using it and see how other people are using it successfully. The tool has four steps, and each step has a set of self-reflection or self-coaching questions to help you uncover new learnings, tap into greater meaning, and make decisions that will bring you more joy.

Part 3 shares powerful tips and strategies that will keep you on the path of personal transformation and alert you when you've gone Off-path. The book concludes with a chapter to help you know if you're using the tool successfully and what to look forward to as you transform your approach to life!

Finally, I need to give you fair warning here. This book is packed with information, laid out in a tight, concise, and pragmatic way. Take your time, reread things, and practice each skill before you read on. Move at your own pace.

I'm not a "sunshine and rainbows" kind of writer. I'm not going to dance around hard truths. I'm going to tell it like it is. Please know that doesn't mean I don't care. I have the utmost respect and concern for you. I've devoted countless hours of my time to bring you this information in a way that you can hear it and use it, all so you can find your voice, find your joy, and live a very different life without suffering, forever. I want this for you more than you can probably know right now. And my direct approach is the best way I know to lay it out for you. I have full faith in your ability to hear and consider these challenging ideas, so navigate them in the best way that works for *you*!

PART 1

The Desire for Transformation

Chapter 1

Meet the Adversity Cycle: Moving out of Ego and into Joy

I'm writing this book to give you a very clear guide using an incredibly effective tool that will empower you to live a more joyful life. I've coached hundreds of clients in using this tool. I've seen the incredible changes they've made in their lives, and I want that for you. And the great news is, you don't need me! You don't need a coach. (Though it does arguably help make the learning process clearer, easier, and faster.) You just need to learn how to use the tools in this guide to become your own coach. Walking the path of the Adversity Cycle will lead to some *big* "aha" moments and help you change your approach to life, allowing you to bring more joy into your life by going to battle with your own thoughts and beliefs that aren't working for you. The essence of this work is that it helps you move out of ego-based, survivalist thinking and into an approach to life that shows you what you need to learn and do to have more joy and fulfillment.

Let's dive a little deeper into what I'm talking about here before we start learning how to use the Adversity Cycle. What I'm essentially talking about is going to battle with your ego.

Ego is a word with various meanings. Understanding your ego, as defined next, will be key to waking up and maximizing the effectiveness of this tool.

Ego 101

In my very basic definition, ego is the armor that guards the beliefs, pathways, and patterns we have built up to protect ourselves, survive, and feel better. It's essentially the part of our personality we have built in response to stressful, hurtful, traumatic, or other negative experiences throughout our lives. We've had bad stuff happen to us, felt threatened or afraid or hurt, and we've created a response that moved us out of that perceived danger or pain. That response is what gets built into our ego armor. It's all the stuff we think and do to make ourselves feel OK, feel better, and feel comfortable so we can avoid pain and suffering in the moment. It's not a bad thing. The ego is necessary.

In fact, from all the research I've done, it sounds to me like it's actually impossible to fully shed your ego. Yet the path of enlightenment seeks to do just that—shed the beliefs that are not true and don't serve us. However, from what I've read, all people have been able to do is be able to separate themselves from their ego, observe it when it pops up, and not act according to its will. But it's still there. So, let's just figure out how to identify it, navigate around it, and eventually stick it in the backseat of the car of life, blindfolded and gagged. Sound good?

So, how do you know when your ego is driving? And how can you identify when a thought you're having is an ego-driven thought and not necessarily something you need to believe and act on? When we are in automatic thinking mode, the ego governs how we see the world and how we react and respond to challenges. On the face of it, this armor protects us from trauma, catastrophe, or unpleasant experiences. Our ego is triggered by our amygdala, a portion of our brain that enables us to feel emotions and respond quickly to negative emotion, including fear and the changes it can cause in our bodies. The amygdala is a powerful database. It signals when we're fearful or when we feel threatened, hungry, or when we encounter other stressors. It also tells us what to do, based on what's worked for us to get out of a similar negative situation in the past.

Preparing for Battle

Our ego wants us to stay comfortable and feel better, telling us that we're OK where we are, that perhaps we don't need to change, that if something adverse happens, we should just try to speed it up, get over it, or extricate ourselves from it. The ego becomes a protective device—a lover, of sorts, of what we consider the status quo. We can't lose our ego. It's part of us. The tricky thing is that we allow our ego to operate like other parts of our autonomous or automatic systems, such as breathing.

The ego helps us survive. However, engaging in challenges—what I call Key Moments—is antithetical to what our egos want us to do. So I'm encouraging you—actually, I'm downright urging you—to take on your ego as you start to use the Adversity Cycle.

At first you'll experience confusion, and you may even struggle to challenge the messages that your ego has conveyed. I'm asking you to lower your defenses and go with me on this. Ask yourself why you would ever want to subject yourself to such unpleasantness.

These patterns, ingrained in our egos, were created in response to past traumas or a survival mode default. It's almost like we're enjoying our misery. The ego wants us to feel like we're in control, like we're right and others just don't get us. Frankly, it becomes easier to let our ego drive while we merely muddle through the issue at hand, without questioning the automatic beliefs and actions our ego is feeding us. Examples of automatic, ingrained beliefs include, "If someone points out something negative about me, they are a jerk," or "When conflict around me gets heated, it's best to just shut up and get out of it," or "This huge failure of my team at work is a result of others' incompetence, so I should just do everything myself."

Even if you're not completely satisfied with a certain response or reaction, it's simply easier to respond automatically, the same way you've done before. When this happens, know that this is your ego protecting you from veering off these deeply etched pathways.

Taking on your ego may be a bit frightening, but you'll be OK. I promise. The Adversity Cycle will help you take on beliefs that you've accepted as virtually necessary to survive and be OK. Think of it as the mental scaffolding that is holding up your entire foundation. What you want to do is collapse that foundation, because its structure is limiting your ability to grow, become much more aware, and experience more joy. Working on building this new foundation can take many years. However, the Adversity Cycle can help you reduce that time down to a year.

But before we start working with the Adversity Cycle, I want you to look at two lists. The first is a list of joyless survival emotions, based on your self-focused, automatic ego. When you read the words in this list, you may realize that you really identify with them and feel some of them quite frequently. The second list includes the joy-inducing emotions that can lead to better engagement with yourself and with others around you. The emotions in this list are an indicator that you are *not* coming from a place of ego, which we will later describe as your "higher self." While you're reading through these lists, let yourself feel these emotions. Think about recent situations that have caused you to experience the emotions in the first and second lists.

You've probably noticed that these are two very different lists. The first list is survival-based, whereas the second list is creation-based. When you operate from the first list, you are in survival mode, which is your ego's response to fear or threats. When you live in fear, your ego is constantly being triggered. The ego has a purpose and provides you with a path to feeling better in the short term, but it will not offer you long-term solutions and fulfillment. Allowing your ego to control your outlook, and even your beliefs, is terrible for your body, your brain, and your life.

When you are operating from the second list, however, you are in learning and creation mode, which opens you up to new experiences and growth. Creation mode allows you to rewire your brain and shift your entire inner world. The last decade of study in neuroscience has shown us that we can literally rewire our freaking brains to not go down the path of stress and survival, so we can more easily access the neuropathways of creation and move toward growth and joy in life!

An awesome bonus to being in learning and creation mode is that your brain works WAY better; your IQ and EQ go up because you are using the higher, rational, analytical parts of your brain more. And instead of releasing toxic chemicals in your body, you actually release chemicals that promote health and well-being—just by thinking rationally, creatively, and with curiosity as opposed to self-protection, stress, and anger.

Survival Emotions (Self-Focused)	Creation/Learning Emotions (Selfless)
• DOUBT	• GRATITUDE
• FEAR	• LOVE
• ANGER	• JOY
• INSECURITY	• INSPIRATION
• WORRY	• PEACE
• ANXIETY	• EXHILARATION
• JUDGEMENT	• WHOLENESS
• COMPETITION	• TRUST
• HOSTILITY	• PRESENCE
• SADNESS	• EMPOWERMENT
• GUILT	
• SHAME	
• DEPRESSION	

Ultimately, the path you choose is up to you. But know this: There are only two paths, one of survival and one of creation. And the Adversity Cycle is your tool to guide you along the path of creation.

This commitment to choose the path of learning and creation and use your Key Moments takes a heck of a lot of courage. In essence, when you do this, you are forcing yourself not to do all the stuff that has made you feel OK for your entire life. You are going to bat against a very powerful part of your brain and psyche, and some might argue, your basic human wiring. I'm not going to lie and say it's a breeze.

In her book *Dare to Lead,* Brené Brown illustrates this commitment concisely and powerfully when she suggests that we all choose courage over resentment. Resentment and regret are sure signs that we've been ignoring what our Key Moments are telling us. Those are matrix-based emotions. It takes courage to embrace these learning moments and allow them to take us to the truth. That is, the truth about who we are and how to live in a way that brings us joy.

This quote from Theodore Roosevelt underscores why taking on our ego is such a valiant effort:

> *It is not the critic who counts. Not the man who points out how the strong man stumbles or where the doer of deeds could have done them better. The credit belongs to the man who is actually in the arena, whose face is marred by dust and sweat and blood, who strives valiantly, who errs, who comes short again and again, because there is no effort without error and shortcoming . . .*

To do the work of the Adversity Cycle, you must live according to the wisdom that you acquire through your Key Moments. Living this way takes discipline and firm boundaries. If you are experiencing resentment, know that it's because you've been busy trying to please others and not doing the harder work to know yourself. Instead, discover and embrace what you need to live a joyful life and commit to living true to that knowledge all day, every day, as much as possible. This work requires that you get good at saying no so you can live according to what's most important to you. *This* is what your Key Moments are trying to show you, each time they surface. And it's time to stop ignoring them.

I have a small example of this ego battle from my own experience as a leader. During my time leading a nonprofit organization, some people who worked with me joked that I didn't seem to possess any emotions. They pointed out that I didn't get upset, and I didn't raise my voice when I felt something was going awry. They said I was almost robotic, especially in times of stress.

One day, one of my team members told me that he finally figured me out! He said that whenever I got mad, I'd ask the colleague whom I was frustrated with to "help me to understand." He was right. I would ask them this to help me to understand why they took that approach or what led to the decision they made. By modeling this behavior, I kept my composure and kept my ego-based thoughts to myself. By inviting this particular colleague to provide more context for his actions (which I may have thought were inadequate or misdirected), I was able to achieve amazing results! I received incredible feedback from him. Instead of shutting him down with a yelling fit or simply muddling through (like our egos would prefer, to avoid conflict and keep order), he helped me to fully understand his thought processes, the information he was using to guide his decisions, and what support he thought he needed and didn't receive.

By inviting my colleague to help me understand his point of view, I was able to see things in a different light. And rather than feeling threatened, I allowed myself to become curious about this new approach. By engaging in open dialogue, we guided each other toward the right process for our company, and we both grew. He became more productive, we became much more aligned in how I could support his success, and I became a much better leader.

This led to a powerful, transformative Key Moment for me in my progression as a leader and as a person. But it really did take me battling away my ego throughout difficult conversations and situations to be able to have the presence to stay curious and sit with the discomfort. It's more than worth it, but it's sometimes really difficult. However, I can promise you, it gets easier and easier. It's a skill, just like any other skill. And the more you practice, the better you get.

How the Adversity Cycle Addresses Resistance and Confusion

Resistance comes to all of us in different forms. And you will face resistance (mostly within yourself) every step of the way as you practice with this tool. After coaching countless people on how to use the Adversity Cycle, I've identified a couple of strategies to help you know if you are on track and how you can stay on track.

The first strategy we call Lanterns to help you shed light on the complexity when you get bogged down, lose energy, or become confused. Lanterns help you see more clearly so you can navigate through the unique forms of resistance that come up in each step.

This is a journey, and there will certainly be many opportunities that will surface that could take you right off course. The Lanterns presented in each step are attributes you can apply to the work so you can speed through it gracefully with clarity and ease. You can meditate on each Lantern or use them as affirmations as you are pondering the questions of each step. If you decide to approach each step with the Lantern attributes for that step, you will be led on a clearer path and be confident that your work is on track!

The second component of the Adversity Cycle that is set up to support your progress and avoid derailment is what we call the Off-paths. These are the most common and fundamental thought or behavior pathways that alert you to the fact that you have *not* really done the full work of that step.

When you have wandered off the path, you should reexamine your Key Moment or adversity through the questions in that step again until you can come out of that work—and for the most part, not see the Key Moment or adversity in a way that shows you are still thinking the types of thoughts that are on the Off-paths.

I've heard just about every argument you can imagine whenever my clients (and I!) are faced with the challenges this tool brings. If you let these resistances, thoughts, and opinions derail you, they absolutely will. This tool is meant to throw you into a battle with your ego, and you currently subconsciously think that everything your ego tells you is not only true but is also keeping you safe, secure, and feeling OK.

Use the Lanterns and Off-paths as your guide: Are you resisting the work or getting off course? If so, it's time to step around those thoughts that are creeping up and recommit to the path that works: the path of transformation.

Your Lanterns of Discernment and Intention

In working with my clients, I've found that moving along the Adversity Cycle is a lot like walking a narrow path through the darkness. Sometimes you realize you're not really on the path, but you don't know how you got off the path or how to get back on it. As you commit to walking this path, the Lanterns can help light the way, and lead you back to where you need to be.

The Lanterns are there for you to use to keep you clear and successful in using the tool. The two main Lanterns I invite you to pick up when you feel yourself drifting from your commitment to do this work are discernment and intention.

Discernment Lanterns will turn on the logical part of your mind to help you learn what the universe is trying to teach you. When this Lantern shines, you will discern the facts and plan a path forward that will create a positive outcome.

Intention Lanterns will help you remember to keep yourself conscious about what is happening moment by moment in your life, so you can see the opportunities for growth and start to catch the bullshit, ego-based thoughts so they don't take over. For most of us—and for about 90 percent of our waking hours—our minds want to be in automatic thinking mode, not logical/active thinking mode. In this default mode, our subconscious is driving and telling us to do all the same stuff we've always done, which hasn't worked for us in the long term, and to believe everything that has been programmed into us that has held us back. This is a huge barrier to progression. If you want to progress on this path, you must commit to being intentional in your engagement with the world around you.

As you experiment with the steps in the tool, you must have an intention to engage your mind and use good discernment, or you will miss it all! It's so crazy, but I see it over and over, and there is actually good science proving that we don't really engage cognitively in most of our lives, most of the time. Brain scans show that most of our brain activity is *not* in the frontal lobe, where we use logic. So we're essentially walking zombies, not analyzing what's happening at any degree of functionality. When this happens, we're coasting on the subconscious.

Believe it or not, we actually have to set an intention to use the logical part of our brain. Awareness and discernment are not our brain's natural state of operation in daily life. A helpful analogy would be to compare your subconscious to your autonomic nervous system. Your subconscious drives your thoughts, just like your autonomic nervous system drives some of your bodily functions (breathing, fight-or-flight response, coughing, etc.). You can intervene with your somatic nervous system, which offers you voluntary control over your breathing. It's similar with your subconscious and conscious, or intentional, thought. You can turn on your conscious thinking to override the automatic, or subconscious, thinking, putting it in check and not automatically accepting the thoughts and opinions it gives you.

Working with the Lanterns

I want you to arm yourself and prepare for battle. I've given you the context you need to start to understand what you'll be up against and the gift of two Lanterns that have worked for me and my clients as we have navigated this often ambiguous and confusing path. I also have a fun little challenge for you! Start to build your muscles now by using these two Lanterns over the next few days.

Each morning, decide you are going to embody discernment and intention in the way you are navigating your daily activities, including the micro-decisions and observations you have throughout the day. Use the Lantern of discernment to ask critical questions about the thoughts that surface. For example, do they represent the path of survival or the path of learning and creation? And I'd like you to use the Lantern of intention to stay alert and aware, so you can *pause* before making any automatic decisions about what is happening around you and choose the path of learning and creation, especially when things don't go your way.

Chapter 2

Time to WAKE UP!

The Big Realization

You can have a totally different life. You can have a totally different reaction to all the things you experience in your day. It's all possible. And the only thing holding you back is *you*. Yep, that pretty much sums it all up right there! I'm asking you to wake up and realize that *you are the biggest thing getting in your way!* Just consider this for a moment. Do you know anyone who complains about their life, but you know they could change their circumstances if they would just change their behavior, or make different choices?

What Do I Really Want?

What if I asked you to tell me exactly what you wanted in life? Would you be able to? Would you be able to be immediate, specific, and complete in your response? Or are you letting subconscious, matrix beliefs tell you that it's not possible?

Our culture is permeated with messages that we should be seeking happiness and wealth. We see images of gleeful people doing all these happy things with huge blissful smiles. The danger in shooting for happiness is that it's fleeting by nature. Happiness is an emotion. So, by definition, it comes and goes.

We've all probably engaged in retail therapy. From time to time we may think we need a visual lift from a fun new shirt or blouse, or we think we just have to have that new tool or toy. And, sure, the blouse looks wonderful on us, and we might feel happy the first several times we wear it. However, if we're still facing a challenge at the office, at home, or in a relationship, that cool blouse isn't the key to long-term joy. The reason for this is simple: External conditions do not give you inner joy. You can enjoy the blouse, but it probably won't lead to inner joy, because it is something outside of you. Whereas a positive self-image based on inner joy lifts your energy and mindset way more than that new blouse.

Happiness is determined by external conditions where we play off other people, situations, or objects. Joy, however, is a state of being. You are likely to experience joy when you achieve a goal you had to work toward or when you experience meaningful relationships and deep levels of personal growth. My introverted husband gains *happiness* by purchasing a new bike. But he gets *joy* out of going on a long bike ride by himself, knowing that he's improving his physical conditioning and health. Making money can bring happiness (and, of course, it's an economic necessity). Some folks, bless them, know how to make lots of money. They acquire things and feel happy. To others, donating money to causes or people in need earns them an inner joy that "happy acquisition" alone may not buy.

Imagine a sales team making a huge new sale to a first-time customer. The team worked very hard with all hands on deck. The sales leader was exhilarated. She exceeded her quarterly quota! However, she had eroded the trust of her team by pushing them to work long hours to *make that sale*, just so she could keep her bosses happy.

There's nothing wrong with pushing to make the quarter. It's a part of business. However, the sales leader was focusing on her external happiness at the expense of the team's collaborative well-being and sense of comradery through long hours, near-term pressure at the end of each quarter, and an eye on the (fleeting) prize. It was a case of short-term hits—happiness—at the expense of long-term joy. We can't always control happiness, but we can claim responsibility over joy. That joy stuff isn't fleeting. It's your mindset and how you experience the world. It's your birthright.

The only thing holding you back is the matrix. Specifically, the matrix of beliefs that you currently cling to that distract you from seeing and embracing your true power and creating a joyful life.

So, What Exactly Are We Waking Up from?

Before we go any further, we must embrace a powerful, hidden force that's been holding us back in the past. To awaken, we must understand it and learn how to fight it. I'm borrowing this concept, with love and permission, from Dr. Barry Morguelan (who goes by Dr. B), founder of Energy for Success and teacher of an ancient Chinese system that uses source energy to profoundly support success toward personally defined goals. He calls this hidden force the matrix. Have you seen the movie *The Matrix* with Keanu Reeves? Basically, the central character wakes up to the reality that his entire life has been an illusion. He's been interacting with the matrix—a computer program that simulates life—that he and everyone else were tricked in to believing was reality. What if we are all living in a version of this matrix?

Stick with me here. I know we're getting a little out there. But here's the thing: Enlightenment studies and disciplines from across the globe have uncovered that we are all essentially living in a matrix—a distorted version of reality. Researchers believe we're actually living in a parallel—similar but messed-up—version that we all accept as actual reality.

The matrix is a complex system of misinformation in our culture that has become a system of lies you have learned to believe and need to unlearn. These lies are about you, the nature of your existence, and the universe around you. Lies like: "I'll never be able to do that," "all rich people are immoral," "I'll never be rich," "people are essentially selfish," "that's just not the way the world works," "life is suffering," or "you need to watch your back or someone will take advantage of you."

Before you get too worked up, you should know that the matrix is a brilliant and tricky little devil. So don't feel bad. It even knows how to thwart the very work of beating it. It doesn't want you to progress. It only wants you to stay comfortable, even if you're suffering and powerless to change your life. This matrix is the dense but invisible web of lies you have accepted as true, and it can often be buried deep in your subconscious. It's the web of lies that creates resistance between you and all the good things you want in your life. These beliefs and resistance drive your behavior when you are in automatic thinking mode (which is 90 percent of the time for most adults). Dr. B is happy that I am sharing how I've learned to apply this concept in my life and the lives of those I coach.

Remember those old cartoons portraying the tiny angel on one shoulder and the tiny devil on the other? The matrix is that tiny devil on your shoulder. But it's invisible, and it speaks to you in your own voice. So you think it's real and that it's you. Because of this, it will try to trick you into old, unhelpful patterns, making you think the illusions are real while holding you back.

So pay attention to the Lanterns and Off-paths in the tool I will share with you. These are your two weapons to identify when the matrix is creeping back in and know how to fight against it and put it in the backseat of your mind and actions. When you use them, you can regain control of your life and drive your way to freedom.

I'm Ready to Drive. So Where Are the Keys?

We're getting there, Grasshopper. I promise, and I love your enthusiasm. When you fully awaken, you will be ready to pick up those keys and drive. And I can't wait for you to do that! In the sections ahead, I'll be guiding you through that very process.

Waking up involves looking at all of the closely held beliefs you cling to. It means being willing to let go of the beliefs that no longer serve you. It won't be easy. And I'm not gonna kid you: Sometimes it ain't pretty. But what I can tell you is that it is 100 percent transformative—if you stick with it.

Here's a personal example to help illustrate what it's like to start awakening and becoming accountable for what is taking place around you. If you've raised a child, you know that you love them with all of your heart. But you also know that a toddler can test you. Big time. In my case, I experienced some pretty tough moments with my toddler each morning. He didn't want to get dressed for school or wherever else we were going. He'd go into a crying fit, and I'd naturally get upset. You can imagine that I felt pretty helpless and couldn't wait for him to go away to college! I was blaming my two-and-a-half-year-old for my terrible circumstance.

But then one day I caught my breath, thought it through, internalized the problem, and changed my strategy. I knew what I was doing wasn't working, so I allowed my son more time to get dressed instead of putting him in a rush where he felt he wasn't in control. I started getting him out of bed just a few minutes earlier to give him more time to get dressed. Or sometimes we would pick out his outfit the night before.

Instead of continuing to sabotage myself by getting upset every morning, I decided to exercise a little emotional intelligence and think things through. By separating myself from the emotion of the moment, I was able to understand and see things from my child's perspective. This is the same thing I do when I find myself in a challenging situation with an adult. I want them to explain their position to me so I can see their point of view. By taking this same approach with my child, our morning routine became *much* smoother and friendlier.

A Little Proof for the Jaded Among Us

Imagine being able to apply the strategy I used with my son to a challenge you might be facing at home, or in a relationship, or even in your workplace. As this example illustrates, you really are in charge of your destiny. You are more influential and powerful than you think. No, you can't control everything. Actually, you can't really control much at all. *But* you can influence your own life and your own emotions and reactions to the events in your life way more than you think.

Have you ever heard the expression "thoughts become reality"? Modern research in neuroscience and quantum physics has possibly begun to demonstrate the mind-blowing possibility of the interconnectedness of our minds and the physical universe. What if we can actually influence physical reality with our thoughts, even if modern science is not fully sure how or why this is happening? One obvious example is the placebo effect, which describes the beneficial effect produced by a placebo drug or treatment, a benefit that could not have been caused by the placebo itself and must therefore be due to the patient's belief in that treatment—or their mind.

There's also the controversial topic in quantum physics called the observer effect. We see this effect when an experiment is set up, and there is a disturbance of an observed system by the mere act of observation. Some physicists believe that one possible explanation for this phenomenon could be that the act of human observation and expectation will influence what is being observed. When the observer effect was first noticed by the early pioneers of quantum theory, they were deeply troubled. It seemed to undermine the existing assumption behind all science of an objective world. What would it mean if the way the world behaved actually depended on how—or if—we looked at it? In reality, scientists have proven far less than the intriguing questions they have raised. Many ancient spiritual teachings and texts from all over the world have taught that human thought and intention has a direct physical effect in the world around them. Like all spiritual teachings that are so far "unprovable" with science, I just consider it with curiosity, try it on, and make my own conclusions the best I can.

Another fun example is found in work done by a Japanese author and researcher, Dr. Masaru Emoto, in his experiment with water. He said negative things in front of a glass of water and positive things in front of another glass of water. The water molecules in the glass of water receiving negative thoughts and words actually became chaotic, disorganized, and ugly. On the other hand, the water molecules in the other container that received praise and loving words were beautiful and orderly.

Imagine how you can change simply by shifting your perspective. Recognize your power and live from a place of power, and you can transform the world around you. And know that you are not alone. The universe is designed to help you learn, grow, and achieve the joy you want. As I like to say, I believe that the universe has my back.

When you shape your thoughts about your life, you shape your present and your future. Think about it. Reflect on a time when you just *decided* something needed to happen, and then you made it happen, despite all odds. We've all had these moments—because we are powerful beings interacting with a universe that is designed to support us, our learning, and our success in creating a life we love.

Take Back Responsibility

The next step in waking up, inevitably, is to claim responsibility. This is the really tough one for most of us, so let's do some digging. What's *actually* holding you back in life? More specifically, what's holding you back from having the most wonderful life you can imagine? Seriously? Yes, seriously.

I ask my friends and clients this question, and they tend to say they don't have enough time, or their life's demands are too much, or they are in an unfair situation, or they are in a relationship that makes them unhappy, etc. Our tendency as humans is to place blame for our circumstances on external factors—factors outside of our own decisions, behaviors, beliefs, indecisiveness, lack of will, lack of self-discipline, and lack of care.

I'm sorry, but that's the most disempowering load of crap you could ever believe. However, your lower self, or ego, would *love* for you to believe this so you can continue to survive doing all the same things you're doing and believing you're just fine and doing everything right. For example, say I convince myself that I'm a perfect boss. I'm supportive and inspiring, and anyone who complains that I belittle them is absolutely full of it. I choose to believe this and allow my ego to protect me and hide the real truth from me—that I have work to do. But it's hard to admit that I'm my own worst enemy, because my mind is hard-wired to protect me from that reality.

Let's get real. How many people have overcome what you are saying is a barrier to your joy, goals, or dreams? How many people have overcome even greater adversity? And who says you can't? Think back to how you've already achieved great things in your life. Didn't you have to take responsibility for making them happen? Didn't you have to drive the changes? Of course you received support, but *you* had to make the decision that you wanted something different—a career change, new spouse or partner, new hobby, new place to live, new work environment, new friends, etc.

The first step to waking up is realizing that you want to have joy in your life and that you are the only thing holding yourself back from that. Then you simply need to take action. You are in charge of your destiny. You are the author of your life story. That's reality. Anything else is a lie you've been tricked into believing. When I started to learn about this and realized how I'd sabotaged my own life, my whole foundation of beliefs began to crumble. At first it was completely unnerving, but it quickly became one of the most liberating experiences of my life.

The Matrix and Self-Esteem

One of the biggest lies the matrix can tell you—the most powerful tool it has—is the message that you aren't enough, that you can't do something, or you won't be good enough/strong enough/smart enough. Unlearning these lies will set you free. And here's an important distinction: Of course there are things you don't know, skills you don't have. Sometimes, you are not the best person to build that spaceship, for example. But the lie of the matrix is about your character. The matrix tells you that you, fundamentally, are not enough. It convinces you that your nature is such that you won't be able to jump that next hurdle or have new levels of joy or fulfillment. It tells you that those opportunities are not for you, because you're not good enough.

To combat the matrix, look at the great things you've already accomplished and think about your strengths. Move forward in the world knowing that you will be learning constantly and making better choices. You will gain skills in discernment, especially using the Adversity Cycle! You can absolutely do anything you want and achieve all the levels of joy you desire.

Working with the Adversity Cycle can sometimes trick people into judging themselves and feeling bad about past decisions or areas where they have been stuck in their progression. That's just mental bullying from the matrix. The matrix wants you to focus on your failures, not your phenomenal successes. I'm not going to sugarcoat this. You will stumble, but not all progress is perfect. Stumbling is part of learning! Celebrate stumbles as signs that you are learning and waking up. Knees will get scuffed, but guess what? They can also heal as you grow stronger and wiser!

Awareness 101

The path you're about to travel down will build your awareness of all the things you've been ignoring or that have been stuffed down in your subconscious. For instance, you might discover old pain (old patterns or roots of behavior) that isn't helping you but is instead holding you back. Awareness is an incredible gift, and it's the key to success with the Adversity Cycle. But there's one fundamental rule we need to really contemplate as we walk this path: **You have to care to be aware.**

When you think about it, you'll realize that you don't become aware of things that you don't care about. In fact, you won't even notice things that don't pertain to what you decide is important and desirable. Caring comes first, so you need to figure out what you actually care about. The easiest way to do this is to ask yourself how you would want your life to look if you could wave a magic wand. What about your health? Your relationships? Your financial situation? Your level of stress? What do you *want*? Or another way of asking it: What do *you* want?

This is a powerful question to ask. I have seen over and over with myself, my family, and my clients that we've all given up on things we care deeply about. That's not how we're meant to live. If you care deeply about having a strong body so you can play with the children in your life, yet you choose not to exercise because you feel like it's a lost cause, you have let the matrix trick you into forgetting what you care about.

To combat this, let your deep cares and interests resurface, and use the Adversity Cycle to manifest them in your life! Oh, and get ready. Because once you're aware, you'll start to see the ugly reality of how each of your decisions has led you straight to where you are now. But keep this in mind: that ugly awareness is power. You can reclaim the power to have what you truly desire only after you see how you have denied that power and let it slip through your fingers.

Waking Up in the Context of Trauma, Fear, Oppression, and Racism

When I begin to talk about how our lives, our health, and our joy are really our responsibility, my clients often get tripped up on issues around trauma, abuse, depression, and oppression of all kinds. I want to note an extremely important consideration here, and I'll elaborate more after you've had more experience using the Adversity Cycle. First we need to make a very important distinction. I'm telling you that you are responsible for your happiness. I'm not saying there aren't a lot of factors out there that are challenging and affecting you in powerful, negative ways. Nor am I saying there isn't any abuse or racism or sexism or oppression of any kind. Of course there is! It's rampant. And I'm not saying it doesn't affect you if you are subjected to these forces. Of course it does!

However, if you're like 99.9 percent of people I've met, you have more influence over your life circumstances than you likely currently believe. And there is way more help, opportunity, and support for you than you've realized, not to mention better approaches you could try. Yet all too many times our ego essentially tricks us into believing that things are simple—that we have no real options and should just survive and move along with our lives. And that simple fact is holding you back.

Our egos want us to blame external circumstances for our displeasure or failures in life. However, that is a disempowering, untrue load of crap. And we all believe it to a large extent, until we do the work of disproving it to ourselves. That is the hardest part of waking up, and the part where I see most people really stumble. So for now, please be assured that I'm not saying there aren't a *ton* of difficult challenges that have a profound impact on you and your path in life. Please also trust me enough to hold on to the possibility that I'm right; trust me that you are probably not seeing where you have an opportunity to have more influence in your life and that instead you are blaming external circumstances and forces for parts of your life that you could actually make much better. It's a hard lesson to wake up to—and also one of the most important.

Waking Up in the Context of Mental Health

This work is inherently focused on your old trauma. As you use the Adversity Cycle, you will learn to look at your fears and where they are coming from, so you can be freed from their grip over your beliefs and behavior. You might come across old trauma that has a lot of power over you and from which you need help to recover. You may be well-served to seek help and support in healing. Our brains have deeply carved pathways created by our old ways of thinking.

Mental health professionals and researchers will tell you there is a symbiotic interplay between brain chemistry and a person's conscious thoughts, feelings, and choices. Many of the symptoms of mental health problems, such as depression and anxiety, become engrained in our ways of thinking, and we perpetuate the brain chemistry that causes depression and anxiety. We actually develop the habit of being depressed, the habit of believing the world is unsafe, and the habit of believing we aren't worthy of love.

Sometimes the best way to empower ourselves and progress along the path is to seek support from professionals, experts, or trusted advisors who have healed from similar traumas. That support can help us accelerate through the processing of that old trauma, to see where it has a grip on us and how we can fight against it. There are talented people out there who have devoted their lives to helping people who are suffering. They come in many forms, including social workers, therapists, energy healers, members of the clergy, shamans, and life coaches, and they would love to help you.

I've used all of these professionals at different times and have benefited from them at various points in my growth and development. Yes, it took some humility to do so, as well as time and resources. But I decided I was worthy of living a better life. I wanted someone to help me through the hurdles that had me stuck. And I hope that you want that, too.

Now, you might ask why there would be a need to use the Adversity Cycle when you could just seek therapy. While therapy can provide wonderful tools to help you cope and regulate your emotions, even therapists can be low on emotional intelligence and unable to teach you how to identify your own destructive, ego-based thought patterns and beliefs. In fact, I've coached many therapists on the Adversity Cycle.

The point is, even after therapy, many of us still need to own and better regulate our emotions and build our emotional intelligence skills. Therapy can open us up for this sometimes scary and oftentimes exciting work. And it can give us the tools we need when we face something that we don't have the skill to address and learn from.

We all have healing that needs to be done, and occasionally we don't have the tools we need for the circumstances that life throws at us. I believe wholeheartedly in therapy, and the Adversity Cycle is the path you take when you're ready to do more than just survive. You're ready to embark on this journey when you want to prevent suffering, grow, and develop your skills at living a great life.

The Path of Personal Transformation

It's important to acknowledge what you're actually getting yourself into when you embark on this path so you will have the context you need to sail through it. I've worked with a lot of people entering the path of personal transformation, and it usually starts with some fairly unnerving realizations, awakenings, and disorientation. Again, we have a choice. We can stay asleep, unaware of what's holding us back, or we can lean into it and see that much of what we have believed is bullshit and wickedly disempowering.

The matrix is essentially the way you are sure what the world is and how it works . . . until you start to see that it's a giant hoax. It is a hoax that most everyone believes, until they do the work of waking up and seeing their lives and the world around them through a different, more honest lens.

This might feel destabilizing. Just go with it. You'll move through this waking-up phase and reenter it with each new layer or realization, and you'll be just fine! In fact, it's quite exhilarating. And you're almost ready! We just need to prepare you with one more big lesson before you'll be ready to walk the path. And that lesson is recognizing that your struggles and challenges are your greatest gift, because they are the fodder for this work!

Chapter 3

Get Ready: Identify Your Adversity in Key Moments

"What stands in the way becomes the way."
—MARCUS AURELIUS

In the course of our lives, we come up against multiple challenges that we may consider terrible obstacles or setbacks. We also encounter daily annoyances, triggering experiences, or just plain old resistance. These experiences are what I refer to as Key Moments. On the face of it, these Key Moments can be uncomfortable, something you want to avoid. However, don't let these potential learning experiences go to waste.

Key Moments represent your chance to grow and progress to the next-level you. A Key Moment is any experience that triggers an emotional response somewhere between "ugh" and extreme suffering, rage, or self-hatred. It's a situation that elicits negative emotion, upset, overwhelm, regret, or resentment. It's suffering or adversity, or even just a strong feeling of not wanting to do something.

We've programmed ourselves to think we can avoid adversity by talking ourselves out if it with thoughts like *Do I really have to do that differently? I'd just rather keep doing what I know how to do.* However, when you think this way, you've jumped back into automatic thinking (or reacting) at the expense of embracing a moment of choice.

We often regard these Key Moments as negative experiences. But a crucial part of working with the Adversity Cycle is to use these Key Moments in a different manner. Instead of seeing situations as negative, I want you to start seeing them as learning moments. Am I saying that life's lemons can be turned into lemonade? Not really. These Key Moments aren't lemons in the first place. They first appear as adversities, but they actually are neutral in that they are providing you the opportunity to learn something about yourself and how you experience the environment around you. In fact, a Key Moment for one person is not at all a Key Moment for another! Your Key Moments teach you a different way of navigating challenges that will work better for you and contribute to your overall sense of joy.

What You Resist Persists

Denial ain't just a river in Egypt. So stop resisting, unless you want a whole lot more of it. It's pretty basic: Either you repeat your lessons and stay stuck in survival mode, along with all the beliefs and behaviors that brought these Key Moments into your life, or you allow yourself to identify and embrace your Key Moments, truly experience them, and yes, even learn from them. Stuffing them beneath the surface and "gritting it out" will only allow them to resurface through the next Key Moment. Usually the action you're resisting the most is the exact thing you need to do to transform the world around you and create more joy.

Sorry, but it's time to start *adulting*. That's the key trait that I've noticed is shared by the most successful people around me. They're willing to do whatever it takes to achieve their goals—even what they least want to do. But I promise you, the rewards are even better than the discipline it might take you to lean right into the exact things you're resisting. The magic about Key Moments is that they show you what you need to do to change something in your life. And after you actually take the decided-upon action, your world transforms, and you learn more about what you can do to create even more joy.

Resistance is related to avoidance. Anything that gets in your way as you're progressing, learning, and trying to reach your goals is a type of resistance. Throwing a hissy fit about these things is pointless. It's the matrix trying to trick you into getting upset and sidetracked from the lesson that's there for you to learn. We actually need resistance to evolve!

It's all good. Just see the nature of whatever is in your way and learn what it has to teach you, and you'll level up in your transformation. For example, when you're trying to peddle on a bike from the bottom of a hill to the top, you're expending energy due to the resistance of the tire on the road, gravity, and the steepness of the hill. Resistance of tires, gravity, and steep hills are not bad. They are the nature of what you will face as you progress. Yet we all throw hissy fits about gravity or steepness all the time, even while they are teaching us and making us stronger.

Please don't wish these experiences away. We need them. The nature of the journey up the hill is *learning*. That's what we're meant to do. And the universe is designed to support that learning and progression. Getting upset is a natural, human inclination. Whenever you find yourself getting upset, just allow yourself to pause and notice your emotional state. Know there's a lesson you might be missing. Let go of the fit as quickly as possible and become curious about what's taking place. Because I can bet you anything that lesson will be gold.

Am I preaching optimism here? Like "If I'm just more optimistic about a Key Moment, my positivity will get me through it. So I'll hope for the best, and I'll trust that everything will turn out OK." Actually, I'm not saying that at all! It's fine to be optimistic at times, but optimism isn't always your friend. It may deny you the opportunity to learn through experiencing Key Moments, diving into the complexity of situations, and using adversity to help you grow. Faith and hope alone may comfort you, but they won't help you learn and grow.

Finding meaning in adversity is a key factor in our ability to overcome huge challenges. We can do this when we choose the path of learning and creation to decide what is meaningful and important to us and focus on that, as opposed to our more basic or egoic instincts. Resilience research has also found that optimism is negatively correlated with resilience! People who can look at their situation honestly, know their priorities, and figure out how to innovate are more likely to overcome obstacles and adversity. However, people who are overly optimistic can sometimes miss opportunities to innovate, trusting that things will just "work out somehow."

Some of my personal lessons on resilience and Key Moments have caused me to stop and think, *Wait a second, that difficult employee isn't a problem I need to struggle through. They're actually teaching me an incredibly valuable lesson.* When I can realize this, I understand that this person is not an obstacle but rather a bit of golden wisdom that I'm being blessed to receive.

I coach many supervisors who manage people. Often a supervisor complains about someone on their team with a "difficult personality." They'll tell me that the person doesn't seem to care about the quality of their work or maybe even about being at work. They seem to delight in pissing people off, or they're just lazy and cynical about everything.

However, labeling someone like that is letting you, as the leader, off the hook. If you use this example as a Key Moment and use the Adversity Cycle to better understand what's behind your colleague's behavior, you'll be able to turn the situation around. Most likely they didn't start off not wanting to do well or failing to contribute to your organization. Instead of merely observing the person through your eyes, take the time to understand their needs and issues, and use this Key Moment to help your colleague. When you do this, you can respond to their needs and melt the resistance that was preventing them from being joyful and more productive in the first place. Suddenly they no longer seem difficult, and you start to appreciate having them on your team.

Anyone up for a win-win?

Leveling Up: The Gift of Resistance

What stressed you out several years ago is not so stressful now, right? What was challenging in the past (early career, early parenting, etc.) is probably not nearly as challenging now. This is called leveling up, and it is the nature of skill development. Stuff in life often seems so hard. Yet we learn through adversity and resistance, and as we level up and skill up, the stuff that used to be hard becomes much easier and then often is not even hard at all.

So, what does this have to do with waking up and evolving? When you wake up and start leveling up by challenging your old ways to live more successfully, you will accomplish even more, experience less stress, and suffer less. You then level up, achieve next-level stuff, and then deal with next-level challenges. These learning moments become war stories in later years when you can chuckle at your old self and how you overcame what once seemed unsurmountable.

However, with this tool, you're developing a skill that will always serve you and bring you greater joy and peace. As an added bonus, you'll experience less stress, and you won't have to wait ten years to see how the negative became a positive.

Stress and suffering don't have to be inherent in your life. That's matrix bullshit. So allow those Key Moments to come into your awareness and consciousness. Be willing to examine them for what they are, and you will learn everything you need to. Key Moments are a gift: Whenever they appear, the universe is showing you what you need to work on to transform your life!

Using the Moment of Choice to Get on the Right Path

To progress on this path of personal transformation, we must not only be able to identify our Key Moments; we must also be able to use personal choice in the moment. During a Key Moment, we often feel intense emotion, coupled with physical sensations such as tightening in the chest, sweating, heart palpitations, pain in the head or gut, or myriad other physical responses.

These strong feelings overwhelm our ability to access the logical, rational part of our brains. When we succumb to them, we are functioning at the level of a four-year-old. I don't know if you've ever been in an argument with a four-year-old, but I have, and believe me, there isn't a lot of complex, rational thought happening. So I'm not going to ask you to step up and be your highest and best self in the moment. That's usually unrealistic. Instead, I'll give you a trick to use to change your thoughts and feelings and interrupt your survivalist thought paths: the moment of choice!

Some of you may be wondering: How do I use the moment of choice? How do I take control back in my mind and body and interrupt a thought pathway that doesn't work for me?

OK, if you really want to know, I'll tell you. But get ready for this, because it's a doozy—I mean super complex. Ready? Great. Here's the trick: In the Key Moment, when you are about to react, do anything other than what you would normally do. That's right! That's it! Literally anything other than your normal, engrained, emotion-driven response. That's all your mind needs for it to go, "Wait a second! We're not going to go down that path! We're doing something new!"

Perhaps it sounds ridiculous, but it puts a little mental pin in the moment, stops old patterns, and allows you to come back and process it later, using the Adversity Cycle, when you're not emotionally heightened or triggered. Going back to the example I shared earlier, when my son was two years old and every morning was a massive battle to get him dressed, each morning I had a recurring Key Moment to practice this moment of choice.

Instead of arguing with him and then forcing his shirt on him, one morning right before I lost my shit, I tried to think of anything else I could do that would be completely different from what I would normally do. You know what I did? I knelt down and asked him if he wanted to sing, and he nodded and asked for the "Itsy Bitsy Spider" song. Instead of the usual drama, we sang together, walked downstairs, and put his clothes on *after* breakfast with no fuss.

This is hard at first. But with practice you'll get better and better at accessing this tool in the moment and avoiding those emotional tornadoes.

Commit to Using Your Key Moments

There are only two paths you can take when faced with adversity, negative emotions, and/or resistance: survival or creation. On the one hand, you can just survive and protect yourself and get through it. Or you can open up to it and use adversity to progress, wake up, and create a new world around you. Neuroscience has unveiled that our brains are either in survival mode (which is most people most of the time) or creation mode. When you're surviving, you're either ignoring your Key Moments or gritting your teeth and steeling through them with your armor up, believing the matrix pessimism that this suffering is just inherent in your life and there's nothing you can do about it. When your brain is in this mode, you have higher levels of cortisol, the stress hormone. Your thinking is more chaotic and disorganized, and it's very difficult to change. But when your brain is in creation mode, it's organized, clear, and focused on what's possible, what you want, and what you *care* about! You can choose the path of creation thinking every day. Every time a Key Moment comes up, remember your choices: You can have a hissy fit and try to survive it, or you can use it to create.

So, now, my friends, I think you're ready to embark on the Adversity Cycle! It's my pleasure to introduce you to this tool and all the skills you can develop through it to help you begin to transform yourself and your life. And now, let's meet our first Lantern.

Awareness: The First Lantern on Your Journey

In this first part of the work, I want you to identify your Key Moments and use the moment of choice. Shine your Lantern of awareness on each moment. Set your mind to be extraordinarily alert, aware, and open, so you will know when you're having a Key Moment. Commit each morning to watching for them. And be willing to honestly view yourself, your thoughts, your emotions, and your behaviors for what they really are. Commit to awareness. It will make the process so much easier and faster!

Activity 1

Practicing the Moment of Choice

For the next couple of weeks, work on recognizing that you are having a Key Moment when you are actually in the moment. Use the moment of choice by doing anything other than what you would normally do. Play with it and have fun! See what crazy stuff you come up with in the moment! And, if you want to go ninja-level with this, you can schedule a moment of choice by planning a behavior you want to use in a Key Moment that you know is coming your way. Perhaps it's that "difficult personality" you know you'll be interacting with next week. Plan your behavior for the moment you know you'll be triggered—and use it!

Regain your power. Use the moment of choice and notice the results.

PART 2

The Adversity Cycle

You did it! Now that you have a solid foundation in the Adversity Cycle, you can dive right in and get to the part you've been waiting for: how to use the Adversity Cycle. As you read the chapters in Part 2, I want you to know this is a path you can take each time you encounter adversity. So use it for your own growth and transformation. Often.

The next four chapters will walk you through each of the four steps of the Adversity Cycle. But remember: This isn't passive work. You get out of it what you put into it. Challenge yourself to follow the instructions and use the coaching questions with Key Moments in your own life to gain experience and skill in the work.

Step 1 helps you step out of the matrix and see it for what it really is. Step 2 helps you find where you have more power and influence. These first two steps will be hard work. These are the gritty, confusing parts that need a bit of determination to get through. And then, you're rewarded by the more inspiring and creative work in Step 3, where you get to tap into what you really want and who you want to be, while gaining some momentum to try new approaches. Then Step 4 takes all the great thinking you've done in the first three steps and brings it into the world, so you can experience something new, and see the incredible, positive ripple effect that different choices and small shifts can make in your life! Sound good? Awesome! Take it one step at a time. You don't need to believe any of it. Just experiment with it. See how it goes and what you uncover.

Now, relax and enjoy the journey. And most of all, don't forget to laugh!

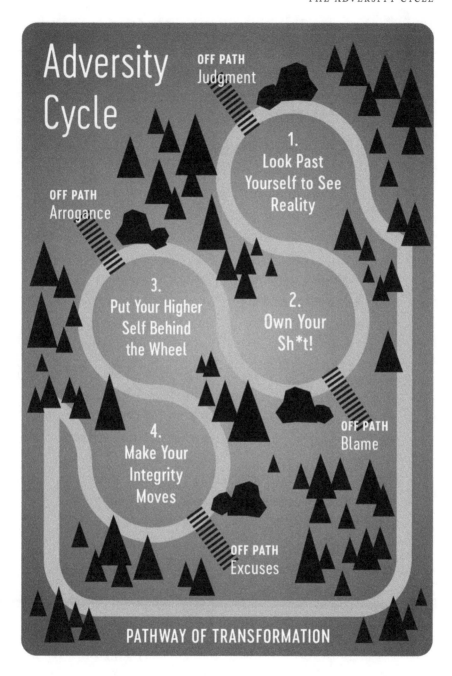

Adversity Cycle Steps

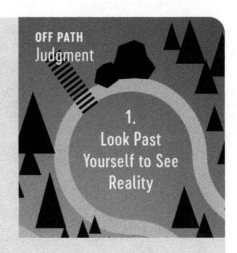

OFF PATH
Judgment

1.
Look Past
Yourself to See
Reality

- Being as descriptive as possible, including the emotions you were experiencing and using the voice of your "defiant adolescent self," describe the Key Moment.

- What is actually happening here? (Think about just the rational, observable facts.)

- When you retell the Key Moment and the narrative you created around it, what thought distortions are you using? (Examples: personalizing, fortune-telling, catastrophizing, mind reading, black-and-white thinking, labeling, overgeneralizing)

- How do these thought distortions shed light on your ego needs?

- Embrace complexity and opportunity. If you acknowledged that you and the others involved are complex, have a limited perspective, and might have more opportunity than what you've seen, what are other elements of the situation you could now identify?

- Using the thought distortions as a guide, name the irrational fears bubbling just below the surface that are fueling your emotions. What's the worst possible outcome of this situation?

LANTERNS:
HUMILITY &
HONESTY

Chapter 4

Step 1: Look Past Yourself to See Reality

Step 1

OK, so we're gonna dive headfirst into the Adversity Cycle with the longest and most complicated of the four steps. I know. I realize this is a lot to ask—but stick with me here. Step 1 lays an important foundation for the next three steps. Luckily you have an experienced coach guiding you, and I'll make sure you've got this before we move to Step 2. Trust me. You'll rock it, and when you're done, the rest will be smooth sailing, because you've already gotten through the hardest part!

What Reality Are You Experiencing?

The first step we must take along the pathway of progression is to understand that we do not perceive a rational, clear, and complete version of reality. Like, pretty much ever. And, more importantly, we shouldn't believe every thought that comes into our head. All those thoughts in our head about "how things are" are *not* the truth. They're just random thoughts our brain is producing. But we nearly always believe them.

Yep, this was a hard one for me to swallow too. If you're like me, you're probably wondering how we can make good choices if we're not even seeing or experiencing what is actually real. Not to worry. It is possible, and I'm about to show you how with some reality hacks that will shed some light on what's really going on.

Reality Hacks

Our brains are wired for survival. I like to refer to this as operating system (OS) 1.0. However, our lives demand a more sophisticated operating system (OS 2.0). Version 1.0 would work really well if we were all still hunters and gatherers. However, in today's world we have a much higher level of demands on our brains and lives, like working together in groups and solving complex challenges. And if you've ever tried to run more sophisticated software on a dated computer and older operating system, you've probably experienced the frustration of the newer program freezing up on you or running slower than usual multiple times per day.

Well, every day, those of us who are still using OS 1.0 are doing the exact same thing as those dated computers. And what I've learned from years of coaching people in this work is that I need to take a minute to help you get out of your own way. So here goes . . .

. . . **You are basically full of shit and shouldn't believe your thoughts.**

I realize that may seem harsh. However, once you accept this, then, and only then, can you engage in Step 1 of the Adversity Cycle. To help you navigate this first step, I've created five reality hacks. Each hack will show you the biggest factor of faulty wiring in your brain. You will learn how this outdated operating system clouds your ability to experience reality and prevents you from seeing the rational, complex Truths in any given moment—all day, every day.

Reality Hack #1: Autopilot

Our brains are lazy. You may have learned about this in high school or college science classes, but you maybe haven't applied it to the way you're living your own life. Our minds are usually running on autopilot, or what neuroscientists call "automatic thinking mode." In fact, we only use conscious, critical, logical reasoning for less than half of our day. A 2010 study by Daniel Gilbert and Matthew Killingsworth tells us that the vast majority of people are in automatic thinking, or daydream mode, for 46.9 percent of their waking hours. That means that most of our behavior—the micro-choices and decisions we make every day about what to do, what to eat, who to trust, and how to approach a challenge—are all habitual and being generated by our subconscious. Our brains are hardwired to keep thinking the same crap we've always thought and function in a way that is not conducive to being fully alert, aware, and conscious all the time. A 2020 study from Queen's University in Canada suggests that the average person has more than six thousand individual thoughts every day. Care to guess what percentage of those are the same as yesterday? In 2005, the National Science Foundation actually published an article stating that for most adults, up to 95 percent of their thoughts are exactly the same repetitive thoughts as they had the day prior.

We are wired to respond to stimuli in our environment without thinking, based on what thoughts have worked to keep us alive so far—not a bad thing in and of itself. However, this means we will keep having the same thoughts unless we set our mind toward being *conscious*, which takes way more energy from your brain. And in a sense, your brain is wired to be lazy, to just keep responding in the exact same ways throughout your day.

This autopilot mode is considered our subconscious, where we hold a lot of beliefs that drive our thinking, emotions, and ultimately our choices and behavior. Many scientists agree that subconscious thoughts can be seen as automatic survival systems that drive much of our behavior. When you live in this autopilot or minimal consciousness state, the matrix is pretty much in charge of your thoughts, beliefs, and behavior. That's not optimal, to say the least! You'll just keep making the same mistakes you've always made and do so unquestioningly, because you're operating out of old, ingrained beliefs you don't think to question. These unquestioned beliefs are largely based on thinking and perceptions from the past that were very limited and often distorted. Pretty darn dysfunctional, if you ask me.

So, here is my question for you: Do you want to be who you've always been and think and believe all the same things you always have? That will just get you the same results you're already getting in your life, right? If you want to level up, open up, get over some stuff, leap hurdles, and experience more joy and less pain, it's time to stop living in the past. It's time to stop believing what you've always believed and approaching everything in the same way you always have. If your brain is wired to think the same crap it's always thought and you keep believing that same crap, you will keep acting in ways that are consistent with your past behavior. And that's not a good thing if you want to progress and transform.

So, it's time to question every thought that comes through that hardwired brain of yours. I do this all day, every day. For example, when I set my alarm, I think, *When do I really need to wake up? Do I really need to set an alarm? What if I didn't? Am I not going to bed early enough to wake up rested?* And then when I wake up, I think, *Maybe I don't need to do the same morning routine I did yesterday. How is that working for me? Is there something else I want to try today?*

And as I start interacting with people, I hear those familiar thoughts in my head: *Great, my son is going to whine about breakfast, and my husband is being overly quiet, as always.* To break the pattern, I choose to disbelieve those thoughts, question them, and live in the present. I may ask myself something like: *What is my son really needing right now? How can I make this morning fun for us?* And then I'll wonder what my husband has on his plate that day and how he's feeling about it.

When these old thoughts resurface, I stay in the moment as much as I can. Old thoughts will always resurface, but I am mastering the art of stepping around those old thoughts and not believing any of them. I know it's just my past and my programmed brain, and I have control. I can redirect my mind in the present from a place of inquiry. And I choose that, because every day I'm remaking myself. I am not who I was yesterday. I also hope I'm not even recognizable as the same person from one month to the next. The practice I've just described is the way you can step out of the subconscious cycle. By just being present and curious, you can resist the temptation to believe all those bullshit, familiar thoughts.

Reality Hack #2: Paradigms

Paradigms are the filter through which we see everything. They are the lenses that color all of our perceptions. However, they are lenses we are not aware of. That's because paradigms are formed through our lived experience—a collection of our environment and experiences and the decisions we have made about life through those experiences—and we accept them without questioning them.

There are four main paradigms:

> **FEAR:** We feel powerless and out of control, so we blame others and seek escape.

> **DUTY:** We have control over our lives by conforming. Thus, we seek security and avoid problems with others.

> **ACHIEVEMENT:** We seek importance and meaning through achievements and project a competent image to others.

> **INTEGRITY:** We are alive and in a state of joy, unconditionally accepting what is, recognizing our numerous choices. We believe in ourselves and care about others.

In case you were wondering, most of us spend the bulk of our lives in the Duty Paradigm. The implications of this are profound. Commonly accepted beliefs and messages in our culture are dominated by Duty Paradigm thinking. These are thoughts like "don't buck the system" or "go with the flow" or "there's usually something wrong with people who stand out in the crowd." Until we start to wake up and see that the filter we've been using to interpret the world is not reality, we will blindly accept the beliefs fed to us by this paradigm. As we improve our emotional intelligence, we spend more and more time in higher paradigms, ascending to the level of consciousness offered to us by that paradigm.

Reality Hack #3: The Fundamental Attribution Error

Psychologists have found that we fallible humans have a *lot* of errors and subconscious biases in our thinking. One of the biggies is this fundamental attribution error. When we see someone doing something unsavory, such as cutting someone off in traffic, we assume the issue is that they have an inherent internal flaw in their personality. We may think something like: *That guy is a total jerk!* But when we do the exact same thing, cutting someone off in traffic, we attribute our behavior to something outside of us: *This guy in front of me is driving like an idiot, and my kid is waiting for me out in the cold.* Our minds have the sneaky tendency to justify our behavior by blaming external circumstances. Unfortunately, they also have the tricky tendency to blame external circumstances for all our suffering, even when it is, in fact, mostly due to our own past choices.

Reality Hack #4: Confirmation Bias

One of the most important functions of our brains is filtering information to shape our perceptions. We receive tens of thousands of stimuli every minute, and we only perceive a few dozen of those consciously. And our ability to accurately perceive those stimuli can be affected dramatically by our state of mind, physical and mental health, and the array of environmental/situational factors happening at the time of perception.

A great example of how this works is summed up in the concept of confirmation bias. Science has proven that our brain actually filters out not only information that it believes to be neutral or uninformative, but it also filters out information that would contradict something we currently believe. So, if you believe someone is out to get you, and you have an interaction with them, your brain will look for facts to confirm that they are out to get you and will literally ignore facts that might contradict that belief.

Reality Hack #5: Thought Distortions

The first four reality hacks illustrate good brain functioning—that is, how your brain functions when it's just doing its basic work and doing it well. Thought distortions, on the other hand, are a reality hack that happen when we are experiencing strong emotions. Modern psychology and research show that humans are meaning-creating machines, and we often suck at it. A great way to identify the lies you have trained yourself to believe (at least partially through confirmation bias!), is to catch yourself using thought distortions, also known as cognitive distortions. These distortions happen instantaneously and subconsciously as you are having a Key Moment. For example, when you get upset by something, you experience a negative emotion, so your brain functioning is actually impaired, and then you place meaning on the situation, or Key Moment, while you are interpreting it. The most common thought distortions include catastrophizing, black-and-white thinking, forecasting, mind reading, labeling/judging, personalizing, and overgeneralizing.

This is a good time to remind yourself of the nature of emotion. Remember, emotions are here to help you learn from the world around you. They are signals, or road signs, on your path to figuring out what you want (and don't want) in your life.

Your brain gives you these emotions to help you learn, develop, and keep yourself safe. True, healthy emotions come in, wash through you, and resolve quite quickly—usually in a matter of minutes. However, they can become distracting and even detrimental to your growth and progression if you hold on to them and place a lot of false meaning on the world around them when you are in certain emotional states.

When we feel threatened, we have a stress response, and that stress response elicits emotions like fear, frustration, anger, insecurity, and hatred. These emotions then pull all the energy of our brain back into our limbic system, or "lizard brain," responsible for our self-preservation. When this happens, reality is distorted, and there is little to no activity in our frontal cortex where logical, rational thinking occurs. Our awareness moves into a state of tunnel-vision. And that's when our ego steps in and tries to protect us and make us feel better in the moment, and, you guessed it, distorts our thoughts. Emotions literally make us interpret situations differently and in a way that is untrue and irrational.

What is causing these thought distortions? This seems like a super crappy trick from our defunct OS 1.0, does it not? Why in the world would our minds play these tricks on us? Why would it tell us, in our most stressful times, that we are being attacked, that people around us are bad, that terrible things are coming, etc.?

I have one simple answer for this, wrapping up volumes and volumes of neuroscience, psychology, and esoteric teachings: ego! If you are having thought distortions, it's because you were feeling threatened or had an old fear triggered and reactivated in your mind. You wouldn't need to label or catastrophize if your fears weren't triggered. And that is precisely when your ego steps in to serve its function to protect you and make you feel better.

Remember, your ego is there because of fear and trauma you've experienced. When you experienced those situations, you created another element of your ego. And most of your ego is in your subconscious. That is to say, most of the beliefs your ego has created (like "I have to be nice or people won't like me") aren't true, but you fully believe them without even thinking about or questioning them. They just hum away back in the darker part of your mind.

However, you have an out. Naming your fear takes the power right out of it. Even just saying it out loud makes this emotional balloon deflate. You're able to pull it out of the darker recesses of the mind and think, *Wait a second, this isn't rational. This worst-case scenario my mind is creating here is highly unlikely. It's just a reflection of my past pain and suffering. It's not real, and it certainly isn't helpful. And you know what else? I'm not going to let it steer my actions.*

Reality Lesson #1

Almost everyone is doing the best they can with what they have. If you are blaming, judging, or making harsh decisions about people and their intentions and their character, then you are not living in reality. You are trapped in the matrix of lies. The most harmful thing we do to ourselves and others as we distort reality is to attack ourselves and others and assume incompetence, malintent, or worse. And that's just not the case. We are complex beings living in a complex world swirling in thought distortion and emotion. When we simplify and distort reality to lay judgement and blame on ourselves or others, we are simply allowing ego to be in the driver's seat. And that car ain't going nowhere but down the same path of decisions that continues to bring us pain, regret, resentment, frustration, and suffering.

Emotions: Road Signs on the Path of Learning

Do you hide from your emotions? Try to blow them off? Stuff them down where they can't upset you? Just try to survive? Do you make emotional decisions when you're triggered? Form opinions about the person in front of you who upset you? Or do you stop and think, *Hey, what's this I'm feeling? Where is it coming from? What can I learn from this?*

Emotions are an unavoidable lens into our inner world. I want to give you some of the most critical information and perspective on emotions I've learned over the years through both coursework and self-exploration. First, it's important to understand that an emotion only lasts a few seconds. An emotion is a physical manifestation of the thoughts in our bodies. We think something, then experience the physical, emotional response. It washes through us and is normally gone in less than thirty seconds—unless you hold on to it. Unless you keep your mind focused on whatever is causing the negative emotion, looping around that topic and relentlessly flooding your body with emotion.

It's also important to understand the difference between an emotion and a state of being. An emotion is fleeting and often out of our control. It's a response to an external stimulus and is dependent on that external stimulus. Relationships, for example, can cause an array of emotions, from rage to glee. However, only you can create a state of being within yourself. Glee is an emotion, whereas joy is a state of being. Joy is a result of cultivation and effort. It's generated from within you, by your beliefs and behaviors over time. Negative emotions like anger, frustration, and isolation are just that—emotions. They are not really you. They are you reacting to your environment. However, joy and peace are states of being. They are a true reflection of you and what you are meant to experience. You bring them about in your life. They are earned and are not a result of something outside of yourself.

The key to working with your emotions is not just being able to acknowledge and label what you are experiencing. It's also using emotions as signs that you have something to learn. Something outside of you is either making you happy or causing you pain. When emotions surface, embrace and thank them—and then pay attention to what you can do to avoid the negative emotions in the future.

Suffering is not a state of being, and we don't need to live there. When we learn how to harness our emotions for deep learning, we begin to free ourselves from believing all the distorted thoughts we have that are causing our suffering. We are meaning-making machines! Our brains are in a constant swirl of thoughts—most of which are frankly quite useless! And when we are experiencing a strong emotion, we create meaning and make decisions through a veil of distortion that most of us do not admit exists.

In the series *Comedians in Cars Getting Coffee*, Jerry Seinfeld says he's learned that pain is just a lot of information coming at once. The reality is that we've all been tricked to some extent. We feel negative emotion when we experience adversity or just plain old resistance when we're trying to make progress. Then, when we experience negative emotion, we immediately place meaning on the situation. The problem is, we place too much emotional meaning on the adversity without first thinking rationally about it. For example, when someone would give me some feedback I didn't like, I would think that either they just didn't understand the situation, or they weren't on my side. The problem with that is that our emotions are clouding our judgement. We place meaning that is inaccurate or incomplete, and then we just believe it.

Wait—am I suggesting that you shouldn't believe your own thoughts? Heck yes! Suspend judgement. Whenever you are emotional, simply put any decisions you might be making about the situation on hold. Allow yourself to experience your emotions and then learn from them later when you're not under their influence!

Emotions are road signs on the path of learning. And "negative" emotions—anger, resentment, frustration, regret, shame, and rage—are actually our biggest teachers. They aren't bad, troubling, or wrong. Our brains are hard-wired to experience emotion. You can act out and resist it, or you can realize that emotions are just your brain's way of giving you information and pointing you in a direction you might not have been paying enough attention to.

If we want to use our emotions to learn and change our lives, we need to acknowledge them, not react against them or make up some story about how we shouldn't have to feel them. They should serve us by enabling us to see them for what they are: signals that we have an opportunity to change. That observation can then prompt us to ask: What can I do to move this situation and my life toward more joy and experience this feeling less?

Activity 2

Time for a little reality check: What is your current relationship with your emotions? Are you giving in to them and letting them deceive you? Or are you ready to learn from them?

1—Rarely   2—Sometimes   3—Almost Always

___I am able to be aware of, recognize, and name the emotions I feel throughout the day.

___I avoid feeling emotional.

___I am good at compartmentalizing my emotions or setting them aside.

___I avoid making emotional decisions.

___I tend to get stuck on some negative emotions and allow them to linger.

___I have strategies to manage negative emotions that work well for me.

___My emotions teach me valuable lessons about myself.

___I have BIG emotions. I've been quite sensitive for as long as I can remember.

___I feel guilty when I have negative emotions toward others.

___ I feel I'm able to handle emotions better than most people.

The first realization we must have on this path of personal transformation is that we have a choice. We can choose to survive adversity and continue our automatic thinking and responses, or we can choose to use emotion (positively or intelligently) for our learning, growth, and success.

Philosophy, ancient teachings, and modern research in emotional intelligence and neuroscience all suggest there really are only two paths: survival or creation. Focusing on merely surviving adversity causes our brain to function incoherently. Focusing on learning lessons to create a new world around us and a better future causes our brain to function coherently.

It's a simple choice. You can continue to perpetuate your past mistakes, or you can learn and respond to them differently. By doing so, you can create new conditions around yourself and influence the world in an intentional way to bring more joy into your life. Pretty effing simple, right? Well, simple to say—but incredibly difficult to do. It's OK. With practice, you will get it. Let this book be your guide. Experiment with this tool. And see if your reality is transformed like it has been for me and hundreds of my clients.

How Do I See Reality in Spite of My Brain's Reality Hacks?

So, what do you do with all of this? I'm basically telling you that all of us have an extremely limited ability to see the world around us clearly, especially when we are experiencing emotion, which is a *lot* of the time. Just admit it. And learn to carry that knowledge with you, even as you are creating meaning about everything. Instead of jumping to a conclusion, interpret what's happening in your day. Try to see the rational, provable reality and know that any other perception or meaning you are creating is probably nonsense! What you are seeing or sensing might be somewhat accurate, but it's likely very limited, incomplete, colored by your paradigm, and *not* how other people would perceive the exact same thing.

Bonus Hack: Get Curious

When you are experiencing a strong emotion, tell yourself, "The narrative or story I'm telling myself is . . ." and then look for evidence that contradicts your ego-based thinking. Get curious and look for other details and nuances that your filters haven't yet allowed you to see. Then use the self-coaching questions in Step 1!

In the personal exploration sections, I will walk you through the coaching questions, as I've done for hundreds of people. But before we embark on Step 1, I want you to think of a Key Moment or challenge you've had over the last month or so. Try to answer these coaching questions when you think about that Key Moment so you can practice Step 1 with me. I'll even give you some common examples of responses to the coaching questions to help you along.

Personal Exploration: Self-Coaching Questions for Step 1

1. Being as descriptive as possible and including the emotions you were experiencing, use the voice of your defiant adolescent self to describe the Key Moment.

To identify the ways our brain stops us from seeing reality, we need to uncover and admit the messages we send ourselves about the Key Moment, along with the meaning we spin about it. In *Dare to Lead*, Brené Brown alludes to this with the concept of the SFD, Shitty First Draft. Whatever story we spin about something upsetting to us is usually a Shitty First Draft. So, let's name it. Get into the voice of your defiant, adolescent self and describe everything you're thinking when you think about this Key Moment.

COACHING ILLUSTRATION

Amy, a senior leader in her company, had an idea to change a component of their services to make a bigger impact to the client, while also creating a more efficient process internally. She brought the idea to the rest of the leadership team, and after a ten-minute discussion, the idea was set aside. The CEO told her, "Think some more about the feedback you heard today, and if you come up with something different, bring it back to us." I asked her this first coaching question, and her response was, "Well, they didn't like my idea, I guess. I probably shouldn't be so upset." I prompted her again and asked her to really get into that defiant voice and tell me everything going on in the back of her mind. She replied, "Well, I guess I'm kind of thinking that they are shortsighted. And I'm the only woman in the room, so I think I have to work harder to get my ideas accepted just because I'm a woman. Also, I wonder whether the CEO even thinks I'm competent if he would so quickly dismiss a great idea without really hearing me out. And now that I'm thinking of it, I'm pissed that none of my colleagues had my back! Two of them agreed this was a great idea before the meeting and then said nothing in the meeting when the idea was getting shot down! They are such cowards!"

2. **What is actually happening here? (Just include the rational, observable facts.)**

OK, so now that we've gotten that out, let's try to strip away all the aspects of the previous SFD that are not grounded in rational, observable reality and record only the facts, like a robot would when reporting about the situation.

COACHING ILLUSTRATION

I asked Amy this coaching question, and she replied, "I guess I don't actually know for sure why my colleagues didn't speak up. Maybe they changed their minds? Also, it's hard to say if me being female played any part in this. Maybe I just didn't present the idea in a way that was clear and compelling. Really, all I know is that I had an idea I was excited about, I got some feedback—and some of it actually included some good points I hadn't even considered—and then I was asked to think more about it. My idea wasn't outright rejected as I've been thinking. It just wasn't as well received as I'd hoped."

Amy did a great job reporting the facts. So, what about you? Can you observe your Key Moment and state only what is known and rational? After you do that, identify the unanswered questions you still have about the Key Moment. Finally, you'll be ready to move on to the next question.

3. **When I retell the Key Moment and the narrative I create around it, what thought distortions am I using?**

Examples: personalizing, fortune-telling, catastrophizing, mind reading, black-and-white thinking, labeling, and overgeneralizing.
Remember these tricky little thought distortions we discussed? Well, here's our chance to weed them out of our SFD and call bullshit on them! Replay your narrative, or SFD, in your head and pick out the thought distortions. This is easier for some people than others. If it's challenging, look at your narrative as just that—a story you should try to poke holes in. You will find the holes by identifying the thought distortions, even if part of you still believes them.

COACHING ILLUSTRATION

In Amy's case, she was able to identify that she was using several thought distortions. She saw that she was using the labeling distortion when she labeled her colleagues as shortsighted. She also did this when she labeled them as somewhat sexist, because she was accusing them of not listening to her because she was a woman. She then saw that she was personalizing when she worried the CEO didn't think she was competent. He had said nothing of the sort, and she actually had no reason to believe that. I prompted her to consider if she was using the black-and-white thinking distortion. She thought for a second and said, "Oh, ha! Yes! I was basically thinking that if they didn't agree with me, they were dumb. That it was my way or the highway! But in reality I have the seed of a good idea and could use their input and perspective to make it more complete and actually better for the company!"

Just as Amy recognized her thought distortions, you can recognize yours. Challenge yourself and be brutally honest!

4. **How do these thought distortions shed light on my ego needs?**

OK, I admit this one is a little advanced and harder to do for some people. It can take time, but you'll get better at it! Remember, the ego is trying to make you feel better and let you off the hook from having to do some hard work or see things you don't want to see. That's the whole point of thought distortions. They're your ego trying to create a reality in which you're perfect, you're right, and you have nothing else you need to do! But we all know that's NOT the path of success. Instead, how can you listen to those thought distortions and then ask yourself: "How do I feel threatened? Why is my ego flaring up here?"

COACHING ILLUSTRATION

I asked Amy to think about her ego's need to protect her and make her feel OK and how that was directly fueling the three thought distortions she used in her SFD (labeling, personalizing, and black-and-white thinking). To her credit, she was quickly able to explain: "I know right away that I feel insecure when I put an idea out there, so I guess I felt threatened when people were critiquing it. That led me to personalize it and also to attack back and label them to make myself feel better. But I'm not sure about what ego need is behind black-and-white thinking."

I explained that black-and-white thinking is usually our ego's way of simplifying a situation so we don't feel like we have any more responsibility. The problem is that then we don't see that we have more opportunity and influence! Black-and-white thinking is our ego needing to feel superior and all-knowing. It is our need be right and not have to actually admit there is more work to do to really influence the situation the way we want to.

5. **Embrace complexity and opportunity!** If I acknowledge that I and others involved are complex—that my perspective is limited, and that there is more opportunity than what I've seen—what other elements of this situation will I be able to identify?

You know how your SFD included a lot of thought distortions to fill in the blanks and create a fuller narrative about your Key Moment? Let's admit something here: The situation is complex. Your brain doesn't want to admit it, but in reality, you don't know what's really going on with other people, and your brain is filling that stuff in, using its wonderful OS 1.0, including confirmatory bias.

When this happens, simply take a step back, look at the situation, and ask yourself what it is you don't know. Then think about what you should try to actually find out to stay on the path of success and not give up on what is important to you about this Key Moment! Let's see how Amy does with this step.

COACHING ILLUSTRATION

For this step, I asked Amy if she could see that there were actually a lot of complex dynamics at play here, that her perspective was limited, and that perhaps there was more opportunity than her ego was letting her see. She answered, "You know, even the idea I was putting out to the group was really complex, and there would be a lot of complex implications if we implemented it. And we didn't talk about any of those risks or possible benefits. Also, the people involved had varying levels of visibility regarding the situation I was trying to address, so what I was proposing may not have had much meaning or importance to them if they weren't directly involved. And for those who were more involved, they probably could see all kinds of nuances that I don't but should consider! So actually, I have an opportunity here to get more into the weeds with this idea I have. I can get more detailed perspectives and input and reshape it a bit. Also, I can present it in a better, more comprehensive way to the CEO, and if it has enough merit, continue exploring it with the group!"

Can you see the complexity of the situation and the players involved in your Key Moment? Can you see how much you actually don't know about the situation, and find aspects of the situation that you could explore more to find more opportunity? If so, you are ready for the final question in Step 1.

6. Using the thought distortions as a guide, name the irrational fears bubbling just below the surface that are fueling your emotions. What's the worst possible outcome of this situation?

In so many ways, this is the most important question you will ask yourself as you use the Adversity Cycle. Ask yourself what you're afraid of. What is the core, irrational fear driving your emotions? This is not easy for many people, at least not right away. However, like all the steps of the cycle, it will get easier and easier, and you'll get faster and faster at it. When I get to this step in the cycle with my clients, I often ask this coaching question: What's the worst possible outcome of this Key Moment?

That question will lead you to identify the irrational fear bubbling just below the surface. And I mean it when I say irrational. Or, if you prefer, I could say illogical or unfounded. But it's still there, speaking to you, causing you to feel threatened and triggering your ego and thought distortions. Without any fear there, you wouldn't be experiencing a Key Moment!

Being able to identify and name that fear and see it as unfounded is the ultimate step in regaining your power and agency in this situation. When fear is driving you, your ego takes over. And we know where that takes you—back around to making the same mistakes and having the same Key Moments over and over! Let's see how Amy does with this.

COACHING ILLUSTRATION

When Amy came to this final part of Step 1, she paused. She said she didn't think she had any big fears, just annoyance and frustration. I pointed her back to the ego needs we identified in question 4 of this Step. I asked if her ego was wanting her to be perfect, know everything, and have no more work to do in this situation, what might that indicate about her fear? She exclaimed, "Well, of course there's that little voice that I try not to listen to that's afraid! That little part of me is always there, and it's always terrified that I will be seen as incompetent. That's the worst case scenario for me—everyone thinking I'm a dumbass."

I congratulated her and then pointed her back to how she wanted to be right and not see the complexity. To which she said, "Yes, I think another big fear here is that it will take a lot more time and effort if I actually want to solve the problem I was looking at and come up with a truly great idea to solve it. I feel so overwhelmed right now. I think my irrational fear is that I just can't keep all the plates spinning, and I'm going to fail in my job and mess up things I really care about in our department."

Like Amy, sometimes you have to look for clues to find those irrational fears, but once you uncover them, voice them, and look at them for what they are, they immediately lose power. This is all you need to do to be able to sail through the rest of the steps of the cycle and lessen the power of this fear in your life in the future. Just name it and call its bullshit! It doesn't serve you, and it's not founded in a complete picture of reality. It isn't truth. In fact, it's a bunch of matrix bullshit you can now start to disbelieve and be freed from!

Lanterns for Step 1: Humility and Honesty

Remember how we talked about resistance during this process? Well, the most resistance is going to come up during this very first step. None of us want to admit that we're not seeing reality clearly, especially when the narratives we spin are narratives that make us the martyr, making us right and others wrong!

Light up this part of the work with humility—essentially telling yourself things like: "If I'm having Key Moments, that means I have things to learn, and I want to get better at life!"

And make sure you are honest with yourself. Be able to take a hard look in the mirror and say, "This behavior isn't working," or "That was a dumb choice." Avoid saying things like "I can't do this," or "I'm dumb," because that isn't honest. It's a thought distortion (personalizing). Instead, direct your honesty at your thoughts and actions and ask, "Does this really work for me?"

OFF-PATH: JUDGING AND LABELING

Each step has an Off-path, a concept I developed while watching how people I coach, including myself, can walk right off this path or out of this work while thinking they are still on it. What an awful trick, right? This is where your exit paths come in. These are signs that you have exited the path of progression and need to revisit this step using the Lanterns I've suggested.

When this happens, simply revisit your thinking on every aspect of this step. We live in a mental spiral of *shoulds* and often say or think things like "He shouldn't act that way," "I shouldn't feel this way," or "You should do this or that."

Shoulds are the result of judgement. They only result in resentment and regret. If you realize that you're *shoulding* yourself and others, drop it.

For Step 1, the Off-path is judging and labeling. If you are still inclined to judge and label others (making a decision about someone's character or intentions), you are not experiencing a rational reality. You are still being clouded by the bullshit narrative you are spinning. Don't continue to judge aspects of the Key Moment situation by saying things like "Our company culture is just crappy," or "Why should I try when I'm set up to fail?" These are all reductive, distorted thoughts. They do not embrace the complex reality.

If you can look at the people involved in your Key Moment and honestly say, "We are all just doing the best we can with what we have," you've probably done a good job with Step 1. If there is any desire to label or judge people or yourself, or even aspects of the situation, go back and work though this step again.

Need a little more distinction here? OK, judgement, in the way I talk about it here, is not the same as discernment. Instead of judgement, *use discernment.* Discernment is simply analyzing a situation in its complexity to determine the best path forward. Judgement is letting yourself off the hook from seeing the complexity and gathering all the information you need to make a good choice. Judgement is focused on inaction and placing blame outside of ourselves. Discernment is continuously uncovering useful information to bring about new, conscious solutions or a better, more successful path forward.

A More Honest Lens

Here's the good news: Step 1 is the longest, hardest, and most complex step, and you just completed it! Spend some time on this one and practice the coaching questions on a few different kinds of Key Moments (e.g., I woke up late for work, my friend canceled our time together without a reason, my house is a mess, etc.) so you get a solid feel for how to really apply them diligently. Use the questions to identify and step around your ego-based thinking. Then and only then, will you see the actual adversity for what it is, in its complexity, through a rational lens.

Don't you want to deal with what's actually happening and not what you're making up? Step 1 empowers you to see your life through a more honest, analytical lens so you can move through the rest of the three steps and decide what you want to do about it!

I've had so many clients tell me they spend months engaged with an inner dialogue with themselves, using the questions in Step 1 to examine everything they are thinking. They see how their thought distortions are nearly continual and also have themes. This is such an incredibly important set of skills to master on the path of personal transformation.

Remember, you don't need to believe the bullshit narrative your brain is spinning. It's been wired to think the same stuff and use the same distortions and flawed thinking. But you don't have to believe it! The most liberating lesson I've ever learned in my life was that I am fundamentally full of shit. Nearly all the opinions I have are crap—needless crap that confuses me and knocks me off track. There's no need for any of it, and it's all distorted and crazy anyway!

If you notice this, just let it go. We're all a little bat-shit crazy. Just laugh and embrace it. Then embrace actual reality when you can tease it out and see it for what it really is. And now that you can step around that old, ego-driven narrative of bullshit, step around it and move on to Step 2!

Adversity Cycle Steps

2.
Own Your
Sh*t!

OFF PATH
Blame

- What aspects of this situation did you cause, participate in, and/or allow? (CPA)

- In what way were you disowning your responsibility by blaming other people or external factors?

- What is the payoff and/or price you've been unwilling to pay so that you can hold on to your bullshit?

- What is the approach you used that does not usually work for you in these types of challenges?

- Remember: It's not you. You are awesome. It was your approach. So, what approach or behavior has made you successful in the past that you haven't yet applied here?

LANTERNS:
COURAGE &
COMPASSION

Chapter 5

Step 2: Own Your Sh*t!

So, as you've probably gathered from the chapter title, in this chapter I'm going to work with you to really own your shit. Don't worry. We all have it. It's just what's holding you back. So you can wallow in it, believe the lies, and be a victim, or you can change your life. But change requires looking at what's holding you back. And the *great* news is that it's just a whole lot of crap! Step 2 is all about coming back into your power. And the first and biggest step in that is owning that you are responsible for your life and that you have played a *huge*, central part in creating the Key Moment you're experiencing now.

We all know people in our lives who are great, hardworking, well-meaning people, but they just never seem to come out on top. They are not successful in achieving their career or relationship goals, or they keep perpetuating the same mistakes over and over in some area of their lives. Well, guess what? That's actually each one of us. We are all living our lives in that marginally conscious state, where we keep thinking the same thoughts and believing the same crap that has gotten us nowhere. So, in this step, you will reclaim ownership of your life. And unfortunately, the best way to do that is to see how you are actually responsible for the stuff in your life that you don't like: those Key Moments.

Almost all of the bullshit narratives we create have only one purpose: to serve our ego. Think of ego as the armor you've built up over time to protect you from the yucky stuff in the world, including past suffering and hard experiences. Unfortunately, your ego has been created from a very tightly wound web of lies that you have convinced yourself you need to believe to protect yourself. These are lies such as "If everyone likes me, I'll never feel lonely" or "Anyone who says something I don't like is bad, and I don't need to listen to them."

The lies we use to protect ourselves and keep us comfortable and "right" are the very things that hold us back from seeing the one fundamental truth: We are the cause of our suffering, our bad decisions, and our Key Moments. Our ego doesn't want us to see that. The tricky part is that we believe most of these lies very deeply. They have usually been pushed into our subconscious, so when they come up, we don't even examine them. Step 2 is our opportunity to uncover those lies and prove them wrong.

OK, how in the world are we going to do that? Well, it's pretty simple. All you have to do is *own your shit*. What I mean by that is that you should own the fact that you created whatever situation you are in. Whatever your Key Moment is, this is your opportunity to own that *you* are responsible for much of what created this Key Moment you are in. It wouldn't have happened if it weren't for you believing and acting on the subconscious lies you believe that make up the matrix of lies your ego wants you to believe to keep you comfortable.

So, own your responsibility! Don't blame or judge yourself. And don't take it personally. Just look back honestly and answer this one question: What part(s) of this situation did I directly cause, participate in, or allow to occur? (Usually, it's a combination of all three.)

Owning your shit is the beginning of becoming empowered. When you do this, you start to see how you are responsible for how your life is, who you have become, how much joy you have, how much stress you have, and all the mistakes you've made that have caused your suffering. And then there's the moment when you realize that IT'S ALL YOU. Wow!

When this happens, don't listen to your ego. It will try to tell you that it's all outside of you and your control. How freaking disempowering is that? The people I know who love their lives and do awesome things in the world are people who unequivocally take responsibility for their lives—the good, the bad, and yes, even the ugly. They see things for what they are quickly and adapt their approach to get a better outcome. They know what they want and what they don't want, and they adapt their approach when things aren't going well without wasting time and precious energy spinning their wheels, trying to place blame elsewhere.

Activity 3:

It's time for another reality check. I want you to take a moment and think about your current relationship with responsibility. Reflect on the areas of your life listed below and rate your current level of ownership for how your life is going in that area on a scale of 1 to 5.

1—I am a victim of circumstances.

2—I have very little to no influence.

3—I have some influence or control here, but there are equal influences outside of my control.

4—I am very responsible for most aspects of this part of my life.

5—Through my choices, I am the author of this part of my life and how it goes.

___My physical health

___My relationship with my partner/significant other

___My current financial well-being and financial future

continued

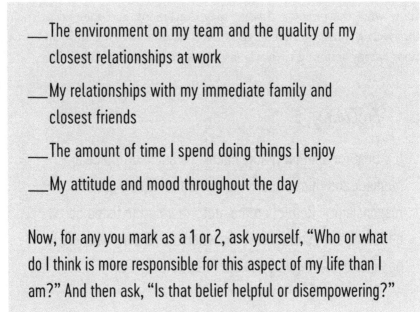

___The environment on my team and the quality of my closest relationships at work

___My relationships with my immediate family and closest friends

___The amount of time I spend doing things I enjoy

___My attitude and mood throughout the day

Now, for any you mark as a 1 or 2, ask yourself, "Who or what do I think is more responsible for this aspect of my life than I am?" And then ask, "Is that belief helpful or disempowering?"

The great news is you have so much more influence than your ego wants you to believe. You are powerful. You are creating the world around you. Empowerment is owning that and shifting your choices accordingly. Still not convinced? Use the Adversity Cycle and prove it to yourself. With practice, you will start to see just how much power and influence you have on your life.

Finding Your Power

If you knew how powerful you were, how much good you could do in the world around you, and how much abundance and joy you could create in your life, it might terrify you. What if all this suffering and frustration were totally unnecessary, and you actually had the power right now, this very day, to change the course of your life forever, start living in a place of joy, and have a powerful, positive influence on those around you?

Wouldn't it be awful to think that you've missed out on all of that so far in your life? Wouldn't that be tragic? Well, my friend, that fear and disillusionment is the very reason your ego is keeping you from recognizing your power. Because once you know how powerful you are, there is so much more on the line. For example, if I'm not being the kind of mother I want to be and my son is struggling, and I know I'm fully capable of turning that dynamic around immediately, I have much more responsibility. If I have all the power in the world to be fully successful in my career, and I continue to fail, that raises the stakes, doesn't it?

Power is serious stuff. Step 2 is all about helping you uncover the power you have. This is power you've given up to other people or circumstances. I want you to stop that shit right now so you can see what you're able to create in your life! Remember, you are on the path of learning and creation, not survival. So go find that power!

In his book *Where Do We Go From Here: Chaos or Community*, Dr. Martin Luther King Jr. wrote that, "Power without love is reckless and abusive, and love without power is sentimental and anemic. Power at its best is love implementing the demands of justice, and justice at its best is power correcting everything that stands against love." Let's use Step 2 to not only find your power but also to use it wisely so you can do what's right for you in your life. And then, as you find your power by gaining the skills in Step 2, you will use Steps 3 and 4 to help you identify where you want to direct your power to create more love and joy around you.

Remember, the matrix wants you to think you are powerless. This invisible subconscious force field against your progress and learning is not real, but because you perceive it as real, it's just as powerful as a real force of resistance.

The matrix is woven together from the dysfunctional and toxic beliefs of other people who have programmed you. Because you have been programmed to accept these things at face value, you believe them to be true without questioning them. When I was starting this work, I found that the most insidious of those beliefs had to do with me being powerless. Step 2, when taken to heart, allows you to uncover your power, which might come with some pain. When I realized how much I was giving away my power by blaming other people or my life circumstances, I was so angry at all the opportunity I'd lost and the suffering I needlessly experienced. In Step 2 you will learn to take your power back, every day, and it starts with identifying where you've let it be taken away from you.

Personal Exploration: Self-Coaching Questions for Step 2

1. **What aspects of this situation did I cause, participate in, or allow to occur? (CPA).**

Replay the scenario of another Key Moment you would like to work on and think about the complex factors that led to that Key Moment. Own the fact that you created *much* of the situation with your past behaviors leading up to this moment. It wouldn't have happened if not for you believing and acting on those subconscious lies your protective ego wants you to believe to keep you comfortable. *Own* your responsibility! Don't blame or judge yourself. Don't take any of this process personally. Just look back honestly and answer this question: What aspects of this situation did I cause directly, participate in, or allow to occur? In my work with clients, we work on memorizing the acronym CPA to help apply this method right in the moment; what about this situation did I Cause, Participate in, or Allow to occur? (CPA!)

COACHING ILLUSTRATION

For Step 2, we're going to follow the journey a client of mine took when working on this step. Brad was an executive who worked long hours. He and his wife would make meal plans for the week, and he would make sure dinner was on the table three nights a week. However, after dinner, there was always a struggle among him and his wife and teenage son around who would do dishes. There were almost always dirty dishes covering the counter and filling the sink. Additionally, while Brad was a fairly tidy person, his son was his polar opposite when it came to neatness. Brad would come home to find his son's things thrown around carelessly all over the house. This was pretty much a daily occurrence. And being a neatnik, this was a pretty frustrating situation for Brad.

After walking him through Step 1, I asked Brad how he caused, participated in, or allowed this situation to occur. He was hesitant at first, saying he had been very proactive about doing his share at home, despite the fact that he worked much longer hours than anyone else. To help shine some light on his behavior, I shifted the focus to his past behaviors that led up to the situation, and he said, "Well, OK, I guess when my son was younger, I just excused his messiness as an age thing, and I've let it go way too long. I'm not holding him accountable. I'm just complaining to him. I also haven't ever really sat down with my wife to talk about how I feel about how messy the house is. I'm just assuming she knows and doesn't care. But I haven't talked to her about a strategy to get better about the situation with the dishes or our son's messiness. I guess I've allowed this to occur with my son, and I've participated in the dirty dishes situation by not being more proactive and just assuming my wife should step up and do the dishes since I'm working longer hours than she is."

By looking back on past instances, Brad was able to nail it. Now it's your turn! Can you examine all your beliefs and behaviors leading up to your Key Moment, including the things you chose not to do or address, and name the numerous ways you caused the situation, participated in it, or allowed it to occur?

2. **In what way was I disowning my responsibility by blaming other people or external factors?**

This is where we examine and identify how our ego has been letting us off the hook by blaming external circumstances. For all the aspects of the situation you identified in the last coaching question, now it's time to identify where you were placing blame inappropriately.

COACHING ILLUSTRATION

When I asked Brad this question, he was very quick to respond! "Oh yeah, I am completely blaming my wife and son. No doubt about it. And when it's my stuff lying around, I blame my chaotic work life, but I am the one choosing to work long hours much of the time. I blame my wife for not doing the dishes, and I actually blame her for not holding our son more accountable for his messiness, since she is home more. But all of that is kind of true, isn't it? I mean, aren't they also responsible?"

I agreed that we are all responsible for our own behavior in the end, but I added that situations like this are not that simple. I told Brad that if he doesn't like how things are in his house, and he has a relationship with the people involved, then he needs to take responsibility for his voice and his preferences and start taking action. For example, do they even know that he's not happy with the state of the house? Do they think it's fine? Has he tried to understand their perspective and work with them on it? When pressed, Brad acknowledged that I was right and that he just hadn't wanted to take the time or energy to deal with it. And then he accepted (and I was proud of him for this) that it was really on him to do that.

3. **What is the payoff and/or price I've been unwilling to pay so I can hold on to my bullshit?**

If you really want to go ninja on this step and see how the matrix is tricking you so you can unhook yourself from it, you want to pay close attention to this question and reflect with brutal honesty. A payoff is a short-term reward for the approach you have been taking, and a price is usually some action you don't want to take, or a belief you don't want to let go of, so you can justify your current perspective and approach.

The payoffs and prices feel good in the short term. They are gratifying to your ego, but they just aren't working for you anymore. Remember, you are actually more influential in this situation than you realize, and the payoff or price you're unwilling to pay is the key to unlocking the truth about why you're not taking initiative or agency in this situation. It's a trick! Once you identify it, you can be released from its grasp on your life and reclaim your power.

COACHING ILLUSTRATION

Brad thought about this question for a few minutes. He finally lowered his head and said, "I really don't want to admit this, but if I'm really honest with myself, I would have to say that there was both a payoff and a price for how I've been acting toward this ongoing Key Moment situation. My payoff is that I get to be the victim and not take any responsibility for the house. I've been saying, 'Hey, I do so much, they should know the rest is up to them.' I haven't been willing to pay the price of just taking the time and having the humility to sit down with my wife and admit that we haven't been doing a good job helping our son to be more responsible for his things and more respectful of our home. I like to see myself as the perfect parent, when I know that's never the case with anyone. It's hard to see that our son's behavior is a direct reflection of my lack of attention to that part of parenting. But clearly that's what it is. And admitting that was a price I've been unwilling to pay."

4. **What is the approach I used in this situation that does not usually work for me in these types of challenges?**

After thinking through the first three coaching questions, this question should hopefully be pretty easy. It's essentially asking you to summarize the approach you've been using to address or handle this Key Moment and acknowledge that it's an approach that generally *doesn't work* for you. It's a pattern for you—a behavior, a set of actions or beliefs, or a combination thereof—that you know doesn't work but you use anyway. It's powerful to identify it and name it for what it is: a shitty approach that lures you to use it again and again.

COACHING ILLUSTRATION

Brad was quick to jump on this question. He said, "It's pretty obvious what I've been doing, and it's an approach I've used since I was a kid. I'd feel overwhelmed with frustration, and instead of talking about it, I'd expect people to read my mind. I've been doing that with my wife and son—pretending they should know how I feel and agree with whatever I believe about the house being messy. I don't actually confront it because I don't want to deal with the possibility that maybe I'm not right! So basically the approach has been to expect them to read my mind and avoid confrontation. That's never worked for me in the past, if I look at the long-term results to that approach, so why would it now?"

5. Remember: It's not you. You are awesome. It's your approach. So ask yourself: What approach or behavior has made me successful in the past that I haven't yet applied here?

This is an important one. *It's not you.* I've had so many clients switch from examining their responsibility to blaming and judging themselves. That's not productive, constructive, or reflective of truth. It's just more matrix thought-distortion playing a trick on you. In fact, your matrix of untrue beliefs takes over your approach in life unless you are aware and conscious about using a new, more effective approach.

You are doing the best you can, and life really does throw us a lot of complex challenges that our brains are not well suited to addressing! Give yourself a break and empower yourself by seeing how your thoughts, actions, and beliefs have combined to create an approach that does not work for you in this situation and will not work for you in future similar situations.

Maybe you can even head off some future Key Moments here! (Yes, in fact, you can. I head off most Key Moments in my life just by examining the success of my approaches and admitting when an approach doesn't work.) Once again, just step right around that matrix tug toward self-doubt or self-blame. Most importantly, think about similar situations or challenges to this Key Moment from your past that you have overcome, along with the different approach you used that got better results. Didn't that feel good? Don't you want more of feeling good about yourself and getting the win in life? See, you can do it! In Step 2, we just want to acknowledge the other, more successful approach or approaches here, and we'll build on that in Steps 3 and 4.

COACHING ILLUSTRATION

I asked Brad what other, more successful approaches he had used in past situations when he was frustrated by the state of things in other areas of his life. Brad laughed and said, "Well, basically the opposite of what I've been doing in this situation! Generally, when I'm frustrated with the condition of something that I'm a part of, I speak up and express what I'm observing. And usually others hadn't even picked up on it or didn't think it was as important as I did, which is fine! But when I point out what I'm seeing and what I think about it and the consequences of it, people usually acknowledge it with me and actually thank me for pointing it out. For example, at work we always had this situation with the coffee maker being left on in the evening. I kept going in and turning it off before I left, but I was worried that one day I would forget, and it would start a fire. I pointed that out to my colleagues. They admitted that they hadn't thought about that danger, and they started turning it off. I know that's a small example, but it's a similar situation. And it's a small example, because I didn't let it become something bigger!"

Lanterns for Step 2: Courage and Compassion

This step can become grueling to those who want to place blame for the situation they are in and then realize that a lot of that blame would more logically be directed back at themselves. Blame is always unhelpful and deceptive. Finding responsibility for circumstances is helpful, but for this work, we're only looking for how you are responsible, not others. If you're inclined to place blame on others, you're not doing the work! Remember, this is all about you—you figuring out how to have more joy and less suffering. Blame doesn't do jack for that; taking responsibility for your own behavior does. Your Lanterns for this step are courage and compassion. Courage so you can look at your actions honestly and avoid the deflection of blame. Compassion so you can have empathy for yourself and others, and the ability to focus on what's best for you and everyone involved, as opposed to focusing on blaming or judging yourself or others around you. This work is hard, so lean into courage and love yourself through it. You've been doing the best you can up to now. And through this work, you're raising that bar. In fact, your best is leveling up even as you read this!

OFF-PATH: BLAME

Yep, that's right. If you're still looking to point the finger outside yourself, at any other person or any external factor, you've at least partially missed the boat here. Yes, of course other people in our lives are somewhat responsible for how they are affecting us, but frankly, not that much. And more importantly, you can't change them. You can only change you. And then you can be a more positive influence on others as well.

So for now, just do your work. Look for every possible angle to take back ownership and see how you can be more responsible for the situation in its complexity. Own your shit and transform it. Part of you will always be asking: *But what about them? They are so up in their shit and full of distortions!* Yes, my friend. They are human. And you have always engaged with humans and likely always will, so let's just focus on you and see how that works!

That niggling little thought that keeps coming back to blame other people is a matrix thought. Step around it. Don't believe it. It doesn't serve you. It's distorted, and it's coming from an old belief system hard-wired in your brain that you need to disprove to yourself. After coaching *many* people to let go of this Off-path, I can assure you that if you just push through, call bullshit on your blame, and stop believing the voice that's trying to blame others, you can change your relationships and change the world around you. Just try it and prove it to yourself.

More Good News

OK, my friend, I have some more good news for you! You've done the hard stuff. Steps 1 and 2 consist of the grueling work of battling your ego and defying human nature. And you just rocked it! See, it's not that hard! And the more you use the coaching questions, the easier, faster, and smoother the process becomes.

Step 2 gives you your power back. Step 2 shows you that *you* are the author of your life, and *you* have the agency and influence to change it in fairly dramatic ways. I mean, heck, you had the ability to bring yourself the pain, frustration, resentment, anger, and helplessness of these Key Moments, so you also have the ability to create something different!

The next two steps you will learn are the fun, hopeful, positive, forward-pointed parts of the work. You get to come up out of the muck and learn strategies to engage differently in your life, in ways that will bring you much more joy.

An important consideration to note here is the pitfall of self-blame. I can't emphasize enough how quickly we all can fall into the trap of self-blame, self-critiques, and negative judgement about our value as a person and our skill level at life. This is matrix bullshit. It's a trick.

You've done amazing things. You've had huge wins against all odds! The matrix is always going to be there to try to trick you into believing what is so commonly preached in our society, across all cultures—the idea that you're the problem, not your approach. We are shamed by our parents and teachers, and we quickly understand the matrix teaching that if you do something that brings harm to yourself or others, there's something wrong with you. You're bad, or dumb, or inherently flawed. That's a lie.

Please be brutally honest with yourself when you practice Step 2. Be honest about your power, your past choices and approaches, and how they work or don't work. And most importantly, be honest with yourself about how well you're doing, how much you've learned, how hard you're trying, and how much you're managing and navigating through right now. You're doing great.

The work of Step 2 is the work of seeing where your approaches have led to results you don't want. That's it! Let go of the terms *bad* and *good* and focus on what is getting you the experiences, relationships, and progress you want. Do more of those things and the less of the things that lead you astray, and you'll be on a very powerful and rewarding path! Now you're ready for the more inspirational work in Steps 3 and 4: figuring out what you want to do instead of the shit that isn't working.

Adversity Cycle Steps

OFF PATH
Arrogance

3.
Put Your Higher Self Behind the Wheel

- How would you act in this and future situations if you were living according to your values and principles?

- What is your ideal vision for the important aspects of this situation?

- How would your ideal, higher self respond to this situation if you were living on purpose—being who you know you're meant to be?

- Reflecting on the core fears you identified in Step 1, how could you move toward your vision and take actions that show that your irrational fears are not in charge?

LANTERNS: WISDOM & HOPE

Chapter 6

Step 3: Put Your Higher Self Behind the Wheel

Shifting Gears:
The Brighter Side of the Adversity Cycle

OK, so we are past the toughest part of the tool. Steps 1 and 2 can be really rough for a lot of people. They get easier as you work with them a little more, but let's just call it what it is—work! However, these last two steps are where the joy comes in. They put you back in the driver's seat and help you take action that will absolutely lead to better results for you in your life. Pretty cool, right?

Steps 3 and 4 of the Adversity Cycle allow us to teach ourselves what we want to do instead of being reactive, acting out of ego, and ignoring the approaches we've been using that don't work in the long run. Now that we've gotten some awareness and skill in seeing past our shit to actually deal with reality, and we see our power in creating both the good and the bad outcomes in our lives, we are emptied of some of those old, ingrained behaviors and habitual thinking that have held us back.

But then what? Well, Steps 3 and 4 are where you get to recreate who you are and how you want your life to be. This is the work on the pathway of transformation that allows you to really experience your own awesomeness, believe in yourself, and trust yourself again.

Moving from EQ to SQ

In her book *SQ 21: The Twenty-One Skills of Spiritual Intelligence*, Cindy Wigglesworth parallels the skills involved in emotional intelligence (EQ), with the skills involved in spiritual intelligence (SQ). Steps 1 and 2 of the Adversity Cycle help you to gain mastery in emotional intelligence. Steps 3 and 4 open up the door for you to discover your prowess in spiritual intelligence. In *SQ21*, Wigglesworth lays out a really helpful way to think about levels of intelligence and how we apply them in our lives.[1] She puts physical intelligence at the bottom of the pyramid, intellectual intelligence one step higher, emotional intelligence one higher, and spiritual intelligence at the top.

As we work to master all the skills we need in life, we need to master the knowledge and skills in these four areas of the pyramid, thus creating intelligence. First, there is physical intelligence. This pertains to how well you take care of your body so you have the health and energy you want while avoiding injury and illness. The next level of the pyramid is intellectual or cognitive intelligence. This correlates to the logical thinking skills you have and how well you can figure out what information you need to thrive, learn, and advance in life. Then there is emotional intelligence. How do you identify what you're feeling, use your higher-level brain activities so you're not driven by your lower impulses and fears, and act judiciously and empathetically with those around you? Finally, there is spiritual intelligence. As Wigglesworth defines it, spiritual intelligence encompasses the ability to "behave with wisdom and compassion, while maintaining inner and outer peace, regardless of the circumstances."[2] Sound like something you'd like? Heck yes! Spiritual intelligence is what we strive for in Steps 3 and 4.

So, are you ready for a little peace of mind and clarity on how to live a life of wisdom and joy?

---

1   Cindy Wigglesworth, *SQ 21: The Twenty-One Skills of Spiritual Intelligence* (New York: Select Books, 2012).

2   Wigglesworth, *SQ21.*

Out with the Head, in with the Heart!

Countless philosophers, sages, poets, and now even neuroscientists talk about the head and the heart and how we spend way too much time in our heads. We are way too identified with all the thoughts in our heads, believing them and living by them. In Steps 1 and 2 you've been doing the work of pulling out of the dysfunctional parts of your thinking, or head. Step 1 allows you to see the lies and distortions and how your ego is being triggered and controlling you, and Step 2 allows you to see how old beliefs cause you to use approaches that don't really work or get you what you want.

We are now done with the head part of this work. Steps 3 and 4 can only be done in your heart. When we push through all the "head stuff" (the rattling, obsessive thoughts and dysfunctional beliefs that don't help us to improve our lives), we are ready for the heart stuff. We are ready to shift into a place of hope and positivity and desire for something better for ourselves and those around us. I've noticed that the best decisions I've made are made from my heart. Of course, I turn on my rational mind and use good discernment and let go of the dysfunctional, ego-based thoughts first. And then I sink into my heart and ask: *What do I really want? What is most important to me? What do I really care about?* These are heart thoughts.

A well-known neuroscientist, Antonio Damasio, describes this dichotomy brilliantly in his book *Descartes' Error* when he says, "We are not thinking machines. We are feeling machines that think."[3] And yet, we all go through life treating each other like thinking machines! We appeal to each other's logic, always show up and speak from our heads, and appeal to the thoughts of others, while largely disregarding the emotions of others.

But neuroscience has taught us that we are first and foremost feeling machines in that our brains are wired for emotion, and every stimulus around us is filtered FIRST through the emotion center of our brains. Then we create meaning and make decisions based on those feelings.

---

3   Antonio Damasio, *Descartes' Error:*
Emotion, Reason, and the Human Brain
(New York: Penguin Books, 2005).

When we ignore this reality, we act out of alignment with the way things actually work, for both ourselves and others. Steps 3 and 4 have to come from a place of heart, using emotion to teach us about and what is best for ourselves and others around us.

I can illustrate the head-heart dichotomy most easily with an example I gave my five-year-old son when he started kindergarten. After a couple of days of school, he told me that a friend from preschool approached him and told him he felt left out, as my son was playing a lot with another boy. I asked my son how he responded, and he said that he invited his friend to join in and play with him and the other boy, but his friend didn't want to do what they were doing. My son said that he just kept playing with his new friend. I told him that while that made sense in his head, he wasn't thinking with his heart. He said that if his friend didn't want to do what he was doing, that was his choice. "Yes," I said, "that's correct. But your heart knows that you care about your friend and that he's feeling sad. So if you were thinking with your heart, what would you do?" He responded that he would think of something the three of them would all like to do together. Now, each morning before he leaves for school, I remind my son to think with his head and also with his heart. He knows exactly what I mean.

In these next two steps, I want you think with your heart. That's the only way you will truly unlock the power of the Adversity Cycle and its ability to transform your life.

Who Are You, Really?

No, seriously. Do you really know who you are? And are you hard-wired and unchanging? What forces have shaped who you have become? Who are you, really? You are not your fears, nor are you the lies the matrix has taught you to believe—those lies that make you do things you regret. You are not your ego. You can now outgrow that set of beliefs that you've created and woven together over the years. You don't need the ego's web of protection; it no longer serves you.

I can now identify my ego-voice (thinking generated from my ego) right as it comes into my head. I now know that any thoughts coming from that place are just my SFD in understanding what's happening around me. So, if we've all made all these beliefs about who we are and who we want to be and how the world is and how things work from a place of ego, it's all just a Shitty First Draft! We have created a seriously distorted image of ourselves and of the meaning of life as well as how to navigate it. It was OK. It kinda worked to keep us feeling safe and comfortable. It just wasn't all that accurate. Are you feeling ready to let your SFD go? You are not your ego, or your personality, or who you've been in the past. You are a changing, ever-evolving being.

Some psychologists and spiritual teachers use the terms "lower self" and "higher self." The lower self represents the ego-based side of you that mainly reacts to the external world from a survival perspective, while the higher self is that true you that has never changed no matter what has happened in your life. It's also the part of you that knows what brings you true joy and peace. It knows what you want and who you want to be, as well as how you want your relationships and your life to be. So, yes, you were born with some hard-wiring. And that hard-wiring is a beautifully unique, complex fabric of traits and desires for the things that bring you joy.

Let's talk about how to start to figure out who you *really* are! That is what you will begin to understand when you use the Adversity Cycle over and over and evolve into a whole new awareness. Your essence is perfect and unique, and you have gifts you are meant to give to the world. You are wired to contribute those gifts, and you are wired to experience happiness and joy from many, many things. In the nature versus nurture debate, your core—your true self or higher self—is your nature, your hard-wiring evolving and maturing as life progresses.

If you are a parent or have known someone since they were a baby, you know what I mean. You understood fairly rapidly that this child was born with a disposition, temperament, and inclinations toward things they wanted that stayed very consistent as they developed and aged. This is our true self. Some of us might be driven to learn, others are driven to do physical things, others are driven to sing and paint, and others are driven to figure out how things work. We are all a beautiful and unique combination of these innate traits, gifts, inclinations, and preferences. We all find joy in different things.

For example, my husband finds joy from riding his bike alone for hours on end. I tried it, and it does *not* bring me joy! Ha! I love tasting inventive, decadent food in a beautiful setting. My husband couldn't care less about that. Great food doesn't really bring joy into his life like it does mine. And we are both just fine. Perfect, in fact! Just different.

His higher self and my higher self want different things in life, and we find joy and peace in different ways. The more we listen to our higher selves, the more we experience the emotions and states of being that are brought about when we live in accordance with who we really are. And it's pretty freaking amazing. You've already had many of these moments. Now imagine having a life *filled* with them.

Who Is My Higher Self?

Who is your higher self or best self? And how much do you know about him or her? When I talk about your higher self, I mean that part of you that is wise, in harmony with the world around you, and acts from a place of mutuality and care for others and yourself. It's the part of you that consciously chooses actions that will result in positivity and progress. It's that part of you that lives by guiding principles and values and has a vision for how things could be better for you and those around you.

Bonus Hack: Get in the Driver's Seat

Now that you know who your higher self is, let this part of you get into the driver's seat. The voice of your ego will always be there. And that's totally OK! Just put that ego in the back seat and strap it into a car seat to keep it contained. Then imagine a plastic divider between you and it, like in a New York City cab. Whenever it gets loud (and it will), its attempts are muffled at best.

In Step 3 of the Adversity Cycle, we're hitting a giant reset button. We're resetting who we are in this adversity, away from ego, so we can return to our higher selves. With practice, you will become clearer about who you are, what your priorities are, what brings you joy, and what you actually want in life. My clients and I have found three key attributes extremely helpful when looking for that higher-self approach to the adversity in our lives. They are values, vision, and purpose.

Values

In modern society, we are rarely asked to connect with our values. Instead we are often encouraged to be in a state of reaction. Questions around who we are, what we really want, and what is important to us have traditionally been relegated to the realm of spirituality. There's no need to separate these vital questions from our daily existence, but for some reason our society has, to a large extent, done just that! We end up focusing our time and energy on reacting to the news, our family, and our coworkers. I don't know about you, but when I die, I don't want my gravestone to say, "She reacted pretty well to the stuff life threw at her and survived until she died." Instead, I want to leave behind a clear message of what was important to me, a message you can clearly read by reviewing my actions, choices, and contributions to the people around me.

Our values and principles are deeply held beliefs that align us with our unique, beautiful higher selves. They inspire us to live full lives, and they guide all of our decisions. To learn what your primary values are, take some time to explore what has been most important to you and to your success and happiness in life.

I use value cards with clients to walk through dozens of values to see what rings most true and important to them. The cards display values such as loyalty, love, compassion, determination, intelligence, vitality, peace, and justice. I find this fascinating, because the ones people choose are always *so different*!

Think about what principles or values have guided you and served you throughout your life. And here in Step 3, think about which of those values apply to the adversity or Key Moment situation you want to work on next, and how that Key Moment would look if you exhibited those core values.

The reason I'm asking you to focus on your values is simple. When we are guided by our values, we pull ourselves out of the grips of the matrix and the influence of our ego. Our ego wants short-term relief from pain or to escape. However, when your sights are not merely fixated on short-term survival, values are what really matter. Our higher selves want us to live by our values so we make choices that serve us and are continually learning and refining our approaches. We are hard-wired to learn from the experiences in our lives and live by our values, and we are rewarded with joy when we do. Living in a state of ego-driven pain and escape is not what we're meant to do!

Vision

When we are in stasis, we don't experience much joy. Yet we silly humans tend to keep making the same mistakes, having the same kinds of Key Moments over and over, and believing the matrix lie that there's just no other way. Listening more to our higher selves frees us from this lie and allows us to say: "Well, if this situation isn't what I want, what do I want?" This really shouldn't be such a profound question, but I've found it to be deeply eye-opening for me and my clients.

Here's an example. I kept having a recurring Key Moment with my husband, and I used the Adversity Cycle for months, over and over, going deeper and deeper each time a Key Moment would come up. Finally I realized where I was still in a state of matrix confusion. I had no vision for what I actually wanted my marriage to be like. I knew I didn't want it to be like so many marriages I saw, and I didn't want it to be how it currently was, but I had zero vision for what I actually wanted. So I allowed myself to dream a little. I dreamt about what an amazing marriage would be like, and when I had that vision, I had something to actually work toward. With this clear vision in front of me, I could move out of my reactionary, ego-based place and start to do my part to create a marriage that I was thrilled to be in.

Vision is probably the most powerful force in your life. It allows you to pull yourself out of the matrix and out of habitual, survivalist thinking, and put yourself in creation mode in your mind. You can start asking yourself what it would look like if this were ideal. After all, when have you created something in your life without having a clear vision of what you actually wanted? When you embarked on that new career path, bought a new car, entered a new relationship, made a different kind of friend, or had a completely new experience, your vision is what brought each of these things to you. I'm sure you can think of times in your life when you created a vision and then just went for it. You wanted it. Your vision was clear, and even though you didn't know how it would come to be, you put your mind and heart toward creating it. And it worked! That, my friends, is a pretty powerful tool we can all use more of. I have an ever-evolving set of goals and visions for what I want in various aspects of my life. I try to spend more time inspired and in creation mode and less time in survival mode by focusing on what I truly want. It's that simple and so, so powerful.

Purpose

In his book *Listen to Your Life Speak*, author Parker J. Palmer talks about how to identify your life's purpose. He writes, "Before I can tell my life what I want to do with it, I must listen to my life telling me who I am." I have worked with many of my clients to begin to shape a clear personal purpose statement by first contemplating what they have done throughout their lives that brings them the most fulfillment.

So many of the truly wise people I've come to know connect courageously and unabashedly with their higher selves, their hard-wiring, and their joy. They invest in developing those experiences and parts of their lives that bring fulfillment and joy in the long run, and they've taught me about a very important concept they experience daily, called flow. You know you are embodying your higher self when you experience flow. Often referred to as being "in the zone," flow is found in different activities for different people. You've experienced it, so let's remember it now and let it guide you!

Think back to times in your life, even starting in elementary school, when you totally lost yourself in something you were doing. When you're in flow, you're engaging those unique parts of yourself that are meant to be expressed in the world—from sketching a picture to solving complex technological challenges to healing someone who is sick. Be honest about activities that bring you fulfillment. Notice them, learn from them, and try to take every Key Moment or adversity that arises as an opportunity to express your true self by creating moments of flow and contributing to your life and the lives of others.

You are fully present; you feel sucked in by what you're doing and even vibrant while you are in flow. You experience those moments of elation when you think things like, "Wow, I'm meant to do this. This is part of my purpose in life." These activities usually come more naturally for us than others, and we have more patience for them and more curiosity about them!

These activities draw us in. For some, it could be singing, painting, taking machinery apart, reading something interesting, having a great conversation, playing a sport, teaching something to a child, speaking in front of a group, lifting weights, researching new fashions, experiencing a new place or new culture, cleaning out a closet, or tinkering with complex equipment or electronics.

You get the gist! Look for patterns. For example, are there themes to the activities that have brought you into a state of flow, and what do those activities and patterns tell you about yourself? In Step 3, we want to take a serious, deeply introspective look at ourselves and use the cycle to uncover our true selves, layer by layer.

To do this, simply experiment, question, and approach the situation with determination and curiosity, always asking: "Who am I without my ego? What brings me joy? What am I meant to contribute and do in this life?" Use your moments of flow to teach you the core lessons about who you are and what you are meant to experience in this life and how you want to contribute to the world around you.

Activity 4: Discovering My Higher Self

Your higher self is expressed in your life through your purpose, values, and principles. When I started doing this work, I had to face up to the fact that I hadn't thought much about what was important to me. I thought about it at a very superficial level, without intention or specificity. This activity is your opportunity to do something that the matrix *really* doesn't want you to do—begin to identify more with your true, higher self than your ego.

Take some time to reflect and write your responses to the following questions. Do this now, in a couple weeks, a couple months, annually, or whenever you're feeling like you've made a shift and your higher self has evolved and deepened. Remember, you are an evolving, changing being, so you may need to examine and rediscover new elements of your purpose, values, and principles as you evolve. These questions are highly valuable in this exploration.

Set a timer for ninety seconds per question. Don't overthink it. Just let your thoughts flow and write for the full ninety seconds. This will only take you seventeen minutes. Then take three minutes to summarize your results at the end. This exercise might just be the most important twenty minutes of your year so far!

continued

My Values (How do I want to experience my life?)

1. What kinds of experiences do I want to have each day
   (e.g., love, intimacy, connection, intellectual stimulation,
   physical exertion, play, music, stability, health)?

2. What kinds of big events do I want to prioritize in my life
   annually before I reach a certain age and before I die
   (e.g., travel, child-rearing, adventure, career changes,
   helping others, home ownership, conquests)?

3. What personal values have brought me the most fulfillment
   so far in my life that I want to continue to embody (e.g.,
   freedom, wisdom, compassion, empathy, fun, family,
   friends, harmony, wealth, style, cleanliness, balance)?

**My Purpose (How do I want to contribute to the world
around me?)**

1. What have been the greatest contributions of my life so far?

2. What are my greatest interests? Where am I
   consistently curious?

3. What am I doing when I experience moments of flow or
   losing time because I'm so into what I'm doing that I could
   do it forever?

4. What are my most important personal qualities that allow me to contribute to others?

5. What influence would I choose to have on the world if I could not fail?

My Principles (What are the most important rules for living that enable me to live out my purpose and values?)

1. When I picture myself living out my purpose each day, what principles for my behavior must I embody to be successful?

2. What are the guiding principles of those I admire and those who are also contributing to the world in the way I want to?

3. What principles do I want to exhibit to others through my behavior every single day of my life?

Personal Exploration: Self-Coaching Questions for Step 3

1. How would I act in this situation if I were living according to my values/principles?

Here again, replay the Key Moment in your mind, removing the distorted thinking or SFD narrative, reviewing the approach(es) you used that didn't really work well or even caused the situation outright. Being really honest with yourself, evaluate what values your past behaviors were demonstrating. Were you demonstrating patience or love? Or were you demonstrating selfishness, defensiveness, or apathy? Then ask yourself:

"Which of the values that I hold dear and that I know work for me and others are really applicable here? And how would I demonstrate those values in this situation or Key Moment?"

COACHING ILLUSTRATION

Jennifer was a very highly valued employee in a company I was working with. She was receiving coaching from me, along with the rest of the management team, and she was relatively new to managing a team and supervising employees. She had a *major* Key Moment with one of her team members. Rob had been in his role for about three months and was having difficulty using the client management software the team needed to use to coordinate services and reporting. Rob continually entered information incorrectly and incompletely and was often late.

After using the first two steps of the Adversity Cycle, Jennifer could see how she had not been seeing the situation clearly, had been labeling him, and was afraid of looking like a failure to her boss as a result of Rob's challenges. She also saw how she had been contributing to his struggles, and she realized that her approach was not only not working, but also was creating a situation with a lot of tension between herself and Rob.

When I asked her about the situation, she described how she valued hard work and accuracy and shared that was actually making the situation incredibly frustrating because she didn't see Rob valuing those things. I pushed her to consider other values she hadn't really embodied in this situation yet, values she knew were helpful in situations when she was trying to help someone.

She thought for a moment and said, "Well, actually, I've been most successful in helping my children or my friends when I've used a lot of empathy, when I really take time to put myself in their shoes and come from a place of understanding." She acknowledged that she hadn't done that much with Rob so far, and this value was even more important to her than accuracy or hard work.

2. **What is my ideal vision for the important components of this situation?**

This is a tricky one, because we often think we're answering it when we're actually being too shallow in our thinking. For example, when the Key Moment involves a conflict with someone in our lives, we might think the ideal vision is that we just get along well with that person. I challenge myself and my clients to have a vision that is well beyond ego or survivalist thinking and more aspirational and higher in nature. Push yourself deeper by asking: "What is really bothering me about this, and what do I wish would be different, even if I don't currently fully believe it could be possible?"

Examine the elements of the full situation, not just the most obvious or triggering part of the Key Moment. For example, when I was trying to apply Step 3 to the recurring Key Moments with my husband, I initially just thought my vision for the situation was that he would start doing more of what I wanted. But that was shallow and ego-based.

Remember, our ego wants us to feel better, while our higher self wants us to *be* better! I realized that what was bothering me the most wasn't that he wasn't helping out more around the house (though that was the impetus for the Key Moments); what was more bothersome was that I didn't want my marriage to feel like it did. I felt alone and unsupported. When I was able to identify that, I was able to create a vision for my marriage—what I wanted in my marriage—and began to express that and work toward it, both on my end and by asking my husband to work with me on his end of things.

COACHING ILLUSTRATION

Jennifer initially stated that her vision was to be a great boss to Rob and for him to be successful. I prodded her a bit further, asking her to think more aspirationally, creating a vision for not just the triggering parts of the situation, but for her ideal relationship with Rob, the team, and herself. She then began to describe that something really bothering her was that she wasn't able to figure out how to help Rob, and she wanted to be more skilled in her abilities as a coach and mentor.

We agreed that those skills don't come immediately and would take some work. She went on to describe that in her ideal vision, she would use this situation to build her skills, asking Rob to help her to see how she could support him better; ideally, they would feel and act like a team rather than two people frustrated with and avoiding each other. Finally, she said her vision also included creating a supportive team environment so when one person struggled, everyone wanted to do what they could to support that team member. She acknowledged that this was a truly inspiring vision and something she felt called to work toward.

3. **How would my ideal higher self respond to this situation if I were living on purpose, being who I know I'm meant to be?**

This question is definitely more applicable to some Key Moments and adversities than others, so it can feel a little tricky at first. Also, as you do this step numerous times and come to a better understanding of who you want to be and what you're meant to do with your life, this question becomes more and more applicable to just about any situation. I've helped my clients with this question by simply asking, "What if you were living *on purpose*, being very intentional and purposeful and being who you believe you really want to be?"

In my personal example, I had to think about what kind of a wife I was meant to and wanted to be! I knew I wasn't meant to be a subservient wife, or a passive wife, or a manipulative wife. If I look at my life and what brings me joy, when I find flow, it's often in helping others to see their potential and live it. I thought about that in relation to my husband and realized that he probably didn't like the way our marriage currently felt either and likely didn't feel like he was reaching his potential and being the kind of husband he wanted to be. We had both let the matrix drag us under. And that made me feel a deep sense of empathy for him and for myself. I wanted to help us both realize a new way to be in our marriage and be able to live as the type of spouses we were meant to be. My husband is incredibly patient, industrious, creative, and compassionate. He's wired to be that kind of a husband. I was meant to be a wife that could help him rekindle that within himself. And I'm happy to say we are finally there.

Just as I did with my husband, you *can* pull yourself and others out of the matrix, simply by being who you were meant to be. Imagine that world.

COACHING ILLUSTRATION

Jennifer and I had fun with this one. She talked about how she had always been the kind of kid who was more patient than other kids—willing to get into the weeds and figure things out, and she felt in flow when she was untangling a complex web of problems. She realized that she had been so frustrated with Rob, and so into matrix-thinking regarding his performance challenges, that she didn't even think to stop and take the time to get into the weeds with him, even though she loves doing it!

She started to think about the nature of the mistakes Rob was making, and she got excited thinking about creating a structure to help guide him through the software more clearly. She said she would use the structure to help him identify where he was getting off track or confused. She immediately knew how to live on purpose with Rob and felt inspired to do it!

4. **Reflecting on the core fears I identified in Step 1, how could I move toward my vision and take actions showing that my irrational fear is not in charge?**

This question can also be confusing because it's inherently a challenge to your ego. Here is where we are really putting ourselves head to head with our wonderfully powerful egos, which have been driving our thinking and choices for 90 percent of our lives. Recall that fear to see if it still has any grip on you as you create a new way of interacting with this adversity. Where might you still be holding back, preserving yourself, or playing it safe instead of boldly changing how you're approaching the situation?

COACHING ILLUSTRATION

This one was actually quite easy for Jennifer. She recalled her fear that she would be seen as a failure for her inability to help Rob be successful.

She was worried that her boss would think she wasn't cut out for a leadership position.

I asked her if that fear was still influencing how she wanted to approach this Key Moment in the future. She admitted that she hadn't even thought about asking her supervisor for input or support in the situation with Rob, probably because she was afraid of her supervisor judging her. But when she reflected on her vision to be an excellent coach, she laughed and said, "That's what I *love* about my boss! She has twenty years of experience in helping people be successful, she's been a brilliant coach for me, and I wasn't even going to ask for her help!" She knew immediately that she would be standing in the face of her fear if she went to her boss and explained the situation and her desire to build skills in coaching, and to ask her for support. And that's exactly what she did!

Lanterns for This Step: Wisdom and Hope

Resistance during this step often shows up either as confusion about what we really want and how to even know that, or when we ask if it's really worth it. We often give up on ourselves and our joy *way* too easily. We have been programmed by the matrix and our years of survival-based thinking and habits to just put our heads down and move along. We think that if we do this, things will magically get better—or we may even fail to admit how much we do not like what's happening in our lives.

We are, in fact, conditioned by the matrix of lies to just survive and to not worry about having a bigger vision for ourselves and our lives. Instead, lean into wisdom—the wisdom of being able to think with your heart more than your head. The wisdom to discern what's right for you. Think about it. All the best decisions you've ever made, that bring you the most joy, did not come from a place of survival. They came from tapping into what you care deeply about.

Our culture overemphasizes the head and heady thinking and decision-making. In reality, we need to use both so we can allow our hearts to remind us what we care about and who we want to be and then use our heads to help us get there.

The second Lanterns in Step 3 are the most important, because they offer hope. These Lanterns help you see that things can be different in huge, mind-blowing ways that you probably can't even see right now. Hope will help light the way for you to take those tiny or big steps to think more aspirationally about your life. It may seem daunting. It may even seem unreasonable, but when you anchor yourself in hope for a different future—one in which you don't suffer from this Key Moment ever again—and you learn invaluable lessons, you will be fueled.

OFF-PATH: ARROGANCE

We all know there's a big difference between figuring out the high road for ourselves and believing we're better than others because we chose the high road. However, this slippery little Off-path rears its ugly head over and over for my clients. When we do the hard work of deciding the better path, we inevitably start to say, "Well, why isn't he doing this too? Why am I the only one changing my behavior?"

Remember, this work is not about other people. It's about *your* transformation. Others might not even know how to do this work. (They often don't.) And remember one of the first lessons in this book: Other people are doing the best with what they have, just like you have been doing. Your high road is different from others' high roads. What brings you joy is different. So, refocus on yourself and extend grace to yourself and others. Avoid the trap of arrogance, seeing yourself as superior in any way over anyone else. That's a lie that pulls you right back into your ego, and it's a sure sign your higher self is not in the driver's seat anymore.

We live by the vision, values, and purpose of our higher selves not to be better than anyone, but to be joyful. And we want that for others too! Remember, we were all programmed with silly beliefs in this matrix of lies, and we all believe them and get sucked into survival mode for most of our waking hours. Have compassion for others and know that the hard work you're doing will benefit both you and them. And be grateful for that!

A Different Approach

As you do the work of Step 3, remember that you are essentially building skills for living life from a place of inspiration and truth as opposed to survival and fear. You know how to do the survival and fear path already. That was your Life 1.0. You know what results you get from running that outdated operating system. We are all programmed to do that. Why not experiment with a different approach and develop a different set of skills to use in your new Life 2.0?

Play with your new and improved operating system! Experiment and watch what happens. Notice what you learn about yourself when your higher self is driving. You have so much to offer the world, and only you can truly find and embody it.

After using the Adversity Cycle over and over, my clients often report they are much clearer on what matters to them; they feel more inspired to make those things happen in their lives and honestly admit what's holding them back. The more time we spend with our higher selves behind the wheel, the more badass our lives become. You don't need to believe me. Usually people don't! Just try it for yourself and see what happens. Take the time to be wise and courageous with yourself in this step so your higher self is truly behind the wheel and you feel that deep desire to try out some different actions or even different ways of seeing things. Have a vision for what you want and align yourself with your purpose and values. Then you will be well-poised for Step 4, where you will take action and realize that you are so much more than what you've been programmed to believe.

Adversity Cycle Steps

4.
Make Your
Integrity
Moves

OFF PATH
Excuses

- If you acted from the Integrity Paradigm, what specific actions would you take here?

- How could you face your fear head-on, stand in your power, and move this situation toward your ideal vision?

- Looking back at your thoughts in Step 2, what opportunities are there to take actions that address your responsibility for this situation?

- Apply the Integrity Litmus Test: Will your planned actions create a win-win-win (a win for you, any others involved, and your environment)?

- After you've taken action: What aspect of your higher self (purpose, values, and/or principles) helped you to make the right move? What does this new approach you've taken tell you about what's really important to you?

LANTERNS:
STRENGTH &
SELF-LOVE

Chapter 7

Step 4: Make Your Integrity Moves

Make Your Move

All this sticky, gooey, clunky, grueling, and sometimes fascinating Adversity Cycle stuff all comes down to this: choosing different actions consciously and judiciously so we can learn from the new results of those choices. Please note that I did not say that we take action to change other people or any conditions outside of ourselves. We do it to learn new approaches that bring us more fulfillment, joy, and peace as opposed to the old, ego-driven feelings of insecurity, resentment, frustration, anger, and helplessness. This last step is the ultimate test of your transformation. Can you actually put your money where your mouth is? Can you move from thought to action? Can you truly live up to who you were meant to be? Now is the time to prove that the answer to all of these questions is yes—more and more each day. *That* is the nature of transformation.

What Is Integrity, Really?

The most distilled definition of integrity is simply following your inner moral compass or doing the right thing—at least as right as you can tell—for yourself and those around you. Step 3 was all about forming that inner moral compass and watching it evolve and sharpen every time you use the Adversity Cycle.

Now you're ready for Step 4: taking the guidance from that inner moral compass and putting it into action. This will require you to do some things that might surprise other people around you. They are expecting you to be who you've always been, but you're transforming, remember? You are not who you've always been. You are a higher version of yourself, constantly learning new, higher levels of how you want to be in the world.

It's OK to do something you've never done. Go ahead and say something you would never normally say. You're the new you. And in a few months, you'll be a slightly higher-level version of you (yes, there's a 3.0!), and you will continue to advance as long as you keep doing the work. Integrity is you NOT making excuses or justifying behavior that you know isn't optimal. Integrity is you taking action and expressing the more conscious, more intentional, wiser you.

Why All the Action?

Remember how I mentioned right up front that if you don't actually use this stuff, you won't progress? Well, this is your shot. And guess what? This tool requires action. This final step is all about making a conscious choice to act differently whenever a Key Moment surfaces and seeing what happens.

It's a grand experiment! The only way to really learn the power of this work and see the benefits of transformation is to try out some of these new choices and behaviors to see if they work better. You must act, be aware, and then observe what happens. Ask yourself: How does the situation change? How does your view of the situation change? How does your emotional state change? What are you realizing about the Key Moment, or the people involved, that you never saw before? What are your new thoughts and emotions when you think about this Key Moment? What key lessons have you taught yourself about using integrity in this particular kind of situation that you can carry forward into similar situations?

To break out of those old habits that are reinforcing those old beliefs, you have to act. Thought alone will not reprogram your brain. Conscious action, with observation and reflection about the results, is what rewires your brain and gives you the opportunity to disprove those bullshit matrix beliefs you've held without realizing they were bullshit.

For example, let's say I have a recurring Key Moment around my health and not having enough energy each day. Somewhat subconsciously, I believe that this low energy level is just inherent with my age and that I'm never going to have enough energy to do everything I want to do ever again. Then I use the Adversity Cycle and realize that I wasn't using all the best approaches or really seeing my part in my own health and energy level.

By using the Adversity Cycle, I put my higher self in charge. I start to exercise more; I examine activities that drain my energy and then address them. I use Step 4 to plan out some new behaviors, like holding myself accountable for getting more sleep, reducing the amount of alcohol I drink, and eating a few more veggies. And I started to say to myself: *Hey! I'm back to the energy levels I felt in my twenties! Why did I think I could never have this much energy again? Matrix, I'm calling your bullshit!*

But it took action, right? It didn't just happen on its own. All the work you've done in Steps 1 through 3 prepared you for this. You are more than ready. Just step out there and make a thoughtful, new-you kind of move!

The Integrity Paradigm

As a practitioner of the *360 Solutions* organizational development platform, I've found that the material presented in their Emotional Intelligence curriculum does a beautiful job of summarizing what they call the Integrity Paradigm. Remember in Step 1 when we talked about paradigms, and how they shade or color everything we perceive? As we improve our skills in emotional intelligence, we actually move up paradigms. We spend more and more time in the higher paradigms of achievement and integrity. Remember, 80 percent of adults in the United States live the vast majority of their lives in the Duty Paradigm.

This is where we try to have control over our lives by conforming to what others expect. We are "good" and "honorable" people. We build security, submit to the rules, and avoid problems with others. And most of what we do, we do from a sense that we "should" do it—not that we want to.

In the Integrity Paradigm, we experience the world very differently. We are alive and happy. We unconditionally accept what is, and we recognize numerous choices about how to respond to the events and circumstances of life. We believe in ourselves and care about others. 360 Solutions teaches us that "the main theme of the Integrity Paradigm involves developing both an internal moral compass and the strength to overcome the challenges we face. We subordinate our immediate gratification (Fear), desire to please others (Duty), and determination to accumulate and accomplish (Achievement), to do what we believe is right."

This state of being in the Integrity Paradigm is not something that just happens. We have to work toward it and make progress little by little. The more we act from a place of someone in the Integrity Paradigm, the more we bring our brain's wiring and our worldview closer to this state of being. Practicing it will eventually wire our brains to spend more time here.

In this paradigm, that state or condition is characterized by harmony with the universe, being at peace with our interdependence, experiencing no stress or suffering, and acting from a place of service and goodwill for all other humans. The Integrity Paradigm is characterized by not having the need to label and blame, but accepting things for what they are, accepting ourselves for who we are, and then acting in that space in a way that will bring us joy.

Seem impossible? Well, if other people throughout history have figured out how to spend more and more of their lives living from this paradigm, why can't you? Don't you want that? I can assure you that I'm living more and more of my life here, and it's *soooo* much easier, happier, and more fulfilling. The things that used to stress me out no longer stress me out, because I no longer believe the crap my ego tells me about how I have to live and be in order to be OK. I've moved on. And you can too.

Time to Rewire That Brain

We all know the power of habit, right? Habitual, automatic thinking will lead you straight to what you've already experienced. Those Key Moments will just keep coming back, over and over, and you'll keep responding in the same ways that don't work and reinforce those old thought patterns. And remember, those old beliefs and thought patterns were mostly created by your ego, which was acting out of survival and self-preservation. Your ego only needed to do that because you experienced fear: You felt threatened, and your ego stepped in. And if you've used the Adversity Cycle to its fullest, you've realized how those old, irrational fears are driving your thoughts and actions most of the time. So . . . we've gotta face those fears here in Step 4.

"What? I have to face my irrational fears?" you ask. Ah, yes, young Padawan. It's time to step up. When we let our irrational fears fester below the surface, they drive our behavior. We're basically saying to our ego, "Go ahead, you can drive. I want protection and survival."

But remember, there are only two paths: survival or creation. And to create a reality in which our fears do not dominate us, we must take actions that fly in the face of those fears. So, if you've identified that this Key Moment is bringing up your fear of not being liked or of being rejected, then do something that flies in the face of it. Say something honest and vulnerable that will help this situation move in a better direction for everyone, even if it's something people might judge you for. And see what happens.

We are creatures of habit. Action is absolutely necessary to take—and stay committed to taking—or we will absolutely revert to our old ways of being. It's how we're wired. When you venture down a new path or a new way of interacting in a Key Moment, you are rewiring your brain and creating a whole different pathway for your behavior in future similar situations. However, the challenge is that you already have deeply grooved pathways of all the previous ego-driven ways you've behaved that will suck you back into those habits. New habits are your weapon to fight off the old ones. So it's time to reinforce some new pathways, and—you guessed it—action is the only way to do it.

Use the Justification Flag!

Why wouldn't we always just do the logical thing that would bring a win to us and those around us? Why wouldn't we each individually live our lives by examining what the best course of action is and acting on that and that alone? Why wouldn't we choose to do things that bring us joy, instead of merely doing things out of some sense of obligation?

Hah! Have you seen the news? Have you looked back at your life and all the times you acted in ways that betrayed your own best interests? Have you just stumbled through your days doing what you think you have to do instead of what would be really rewarding or life-giving? Remember, it's not you. You're awesome. It's your approach—you know, the one you chose while the matrix grabbed you by the balls, flared up your ego, hijacked your amygdala, and made you do crazy shit because you had to do something—that is being driven by your hard-wired, subconscious beliefs.

It happens, well, all the time—and certainly more often than integrity-based behavior. And we've all justified it to ourselves and perpetuated these justifications in our culture. Across all cultures and all of history, we have proven over and over that we are masterful at sinking into dysfunctional behaviors that only bring negative consequences for ourselves and one another. We are also masterful at living lives of duty and obligation and never asking, "What do I really want? Is there something I could be doing that's more important to me? Something more in line with my values?"

If you are not focused on being aware of the matrix and being intentional about your actions, you will continue to do things that go against your own values, hurt yourself, betray your integrity, and bring negativity into your life. Justifications, therefore, are the big flag that you are in the matrix, that you are not living according to your higher self.

Common Justifications

Let's be clear about what I mean by justification. A justification is a thought or impulse you have in your head to explain away behavior or choices you make that are less than what your higher self would do. Here are some specific examples from clients and from my own experiences:

1. I don't have time to play with my son, because work is piling up on me.

2. I can't stop and help this person, because I'm already late, and this person should not have gotten themselves into this situation in the first place.

3. I'm yelling at him because he yells at me, and it's clearly the only way he can hear me.

4. I guess I have to do this, even though I really don't want to, because I would be letting someone down if I didn't.

5. I'm too busy with other things to help that colleague/ family member.

6. I'm too busy with other things to take care of myself.

7. This is just the way things are in this company/industry, so I'm just going with the norm when I act aggressively/ compete unfairly/take advantage of people.

Do any of these sound familiar? I used to be quite talented in the realm of justifications, using them way too frequently. I would use the imagined scarcity of time or other people's behavior to make myself feel like my bad choices were OK and really all I could reasonably do in that situation.

When we use justifications, we blame external circumstances, events, or people for our behavior. And we learned in Step 2 that's a bunch of crap! But just watch, you'll slip into it over and over. This is a big trick of the matrix. I see justifications with clients *a lot*. I'll ask them what new approaches they are taking to rebuild a strained relationship or correct a choice they made that they regret, and I'll hear a litany of thinly veiled justifications like the ones above. They might not say, "Well, no one around here steps in to help out the team, so I'm not going to," but they will say, "That's just not how things are around here," or "That's not really how our culture works." And before you start telling me why your situation is unique, I'm going to ask you to take a deep breath and look inward at your motivation for telling me this. It takes immense awareness and strength to call bullshit on your own justifications. I know. I've been there, and I still find myself there on occasion. Just know that you are actually calling bullshit on the matrix when you identify and stop this pattern in your own life. So call bullshit on your excuses whenever you notice them surfacing and make that move into integrity.

How Do I Know I'm in the Matrix?

Now that you understand what kinds of thoughts, beliefs, and actions surface when you're on the path of survival, and you've gained some awareness and skill in living as your higher self, you're ready to answer two basic questions: How are you spending your time? And why? Reflect on your answer to these questions. How do you feel about your responses? If you are experiencing feelings of obligation, duty, and resentment, you're in the matrix. And if you are justifying your actions and choices, you have just betrayed your higher self, which means, you guessed it, you're in the matrix.

To break this pattern, spend your time in the way that your higher self would have you spend your time. Treat other people in a way that's in line with your moral compass. You will be hugely rewarded. It's an existential Truth, y'all. Start to notice when you are justifying your behavior or your time, and see that justification as a big red flag that you are not living according to your moral compass. Whenever you justify, you betray yourself. You do this because you've just deviated from your moral compass, and your ego can't stand to be wrong or thought of as bad.

The book *Leadership and Self-Deception* by the Arbinger Institute[1] lays out this dynamic quite brilliantly. It describes the journey of one man from

---

1   The Arbinger Institute, *Leadership and
Self-Deception: Getting Out of the Box* (San
Francisco: Berrett-Koehler Publishers, 2018).

a place of ego and self-deception into an awareness of his own inclinations toward self-deception and how that leads directly to self-betrayal. As we are learning from our work with the reflection questions in Step 1, it's easy for us to fool ourselves when our ego is overactive and we believe those old, destructive matrix beliefs.

In the book, the story suggests that it's only after we betray ourselves that we need to then justify our behavior, which causes us to sink even further into self-deception. For example, if a colleague could really use my help, but that would mean taking an hour out of my schedule when I'm already feeling overloaded, I might choose to ignore the fact that I could help them. However, my higher self knows that if I were following my inner moral compass and living by my principles, I would stop and help them. My ego has to justify that behavior by creating a narrative of distortion, or deception, to validate my choice to not help them.

Maybe I create a narrative about how they should already know how to do that task or how they need to learn the hard way like I did. Or maybe I create a narrative about how much more important my time is than theirs. Maybe I even become a little bitter that they aren't able to do that task already, so I start casting blame or judgement on them. But what if I would have just stopped and helped them? Would I have needed to create that narrative? Probably not. Tricky, crappy little mind-game, right? And what's worse is that element of confirmation bias jumps right on in there and perpetuates that judgement I've made about them or their situation, and I start to see evidence to support that narrative. I start to notice how lazy they are or how inefficient or slow they are. I start to see all the reasons my time is more valuable than theirs, and I filter out all the evidence to the contrary!

I've seen this take out full teams, get people fired, destroy cultures, and ruin leaders. It's no joke. And we've all done it. And we will all continue to betray ourselves and deceive ourselves when we don't act from a place of integrity. It's not worth it. No need to get down on yourself, though. Since you are living in a matrix of lies and deception, you will occasionally get tricked. Those tricks will lead to Key Moments and adversity, which you can use to identify the trick, unlearn the lie, and avoid that mistake and self-betrayal in the future. It's not that complicated. But how badly do you want to see it? How committed are you to acting with integrity, even when no one is looking?

The focus of the deeper work of the Adversity Cycle is to identify when you are in the matrix. Justification is the most helpful flag you can use. Whenever you start justifying, this is your cue to do some digging.

Bonus Hack: Get Out of Your Head

If you're justifying things, the cure is simple: Get out of your head. To do this, get curious and try to identify the subconscious beliefs that are driving your behavior and creating *your* matrix of bullshit. The matrix has deceived you into believing crap like "Things will fall apart if I don't work my butt off every day" or "No one will like me if I'm really honest about how I'm feeling."

These beliefs have been programmed into you by people who live in the matrix too. By asking questions, you can disbelieve this old programming, live a life of authenticity to your higher self, and kick all those lies the matrix tells you to the curb.

This deeper work allows you to identify when you are not being your higher self and honoring yourself enough to do what brings you joy and fulfillment. This will allow you to extricate yourself from the matrix and see what you really want to do—not what you should or have to do—because it's important to you and brings you joy. There is no joy in the matrix, just survival, and that's not the path you're on now. By choosing to work with the Adversity Cycle, you are putting yourself on a path of learning, growth, and personal transformation.

Justification is a pretty common occurrence. One of my clients needed to have a difficult conversation with her boss. We worked through the Adversity Cycle, and she identified her integrity move as having an authentic, direct conversation with her boss to let him know he had been letting her down in a very big way and that his behavior was affecting her ability to be successful. Each week, I would come back to her and ask if she'd had the conversation.

The first week she explained (aka justified) that he wasn't feeling well, so she thought it would be better to put it off. The second week she told me she wasn't sure she needed to have that conversation now, because she had made a joke about it, and he seemed to get it, so she didn't want to belabor the issue. The third week she admitted that his behavior hadn't changed, but she was realizing that it was really the fast-paced culture of the company that was making him behave in the way that was letting her down; it wasn't really his fault, so it would be unfair to call him out on it.

All of these justifications were bullshit. And somewhere inside she knew it. I simply asked her to reflect on her values as a leader and what she would want her team members to do if she was doing something that negatively affected their results. She said she would want them to tell her directly.

I let her sit with that, and she realized she'd been justifying her decision not to have the hard conversation with her boss. She then said, "I guess what's really going on is that I just don't want to upset him, and I'm afraid he won't like me if I call him out on this. I think I have a real need to be liked that is hurting my ability to do what I know I need to do."

Yes. This was a matrix trick. In the matrix, you believe things like "everyone needs to like me," which is complete bullshit. You also believe that people won't like you if you are honest with them. Also bullshit. But those beliefs drive our behavior, and we don't usually see them for what they are—unless we are engaged in this work. And it is only when we identify these lies that we can be free of them.

My client held a matrix belief about needing to be liked that was not true, and it was holding her back from her own success and fulfillment at work. That is the power of the Adversity Cycle at this deeper level. Once you come out of the distortion and disempowerment by doing Steps 1 and 2, you move into the more subtle, deeper work in Steps 3 and 4, where you begin to really see where the matrix has you by the balls, as well as what beliefs allowed it to grab you in the first place. You see clearly how to refocus on your higher self and your joy to pull yourself out of the matrix of lies that is holding you back.

Tricks and Tips for Step 4

I'm going to go ahead and let you in on a little secret so you're not taken off guard as you start the coaching questions for Step 4. Here's a very fundamental lesson I've discovered for myself and the clients I coach in this step: **The exact action you realize you must take is often the one you've been resisting the most.** It could be something like having a really hard conversation, admitting fault, or possibly putting a relationship at risk.

I get to this step in every coaching conversation and see the familiar look in someone's eyes when they tell me the action they would take if they truly stood in their power and integrity. That look, my friends, is often dread. So let's just admit it here. It's going to be uncomfortable. But remember how you want to stop suffering from Key Moments like this in the future? This action you dread is, in fact, the way. I never said this path was easy. While I don't care about your comfort, I care deeply for your progress and your joy. Your ego wants you to be comfortable. Who do you want to listen to?

I have one final secret to let you in on for Step 4. It's quite simple and quite profound. These hard-won battles of living in integrity happen inside, in a place invisible to others. You'll do all this work, take a new action, and reap incredible rewards and learning, and it's highly likely that no one will notice! So watch for your successes—and celebrate them like crazy! Then seek out someone who can celebrate with you. Share your learning and what you're discovering. These new behaviors will bring all kinds of rewards for you in every aspect of life. But most importantly, the real victory is that you won your inner battle and are strengthening your ability to do it more and more.

Personal Exploration: Self-Coaching Questions for Step 4

1. **If I acted from the Integrity Paradigm, how would I choose to act here?**

Put yourself in the shoes of someone who lives exclusively in the Integrity Paradigm and imagine how they would see the situation in its entirety and what kinds of choices they would make to address the situation and express their moral compass. How would they seek harmony for themselves and others? How would they avoid thoughts and behaviors that were approval-seeking or overly ambitious? How would they dig deep to their core and apply the thinking they did in Step 3 in very direct and comprehensive ways?

COACHING ILLUSTRATION

Alan's Key Moment had to do with his immediate supervisor. She would promise to do things to help him progress in his projects at work and then forget. She was really well-liked by the team, but everyone was starting to lose trust in her and become frustrated. Alan felt like she didn't really care about the team members' success; he wondered if she was just all about herself and making herself look good.

After doing the first two steps of the Adversity Cycle, Alan was able to see the distorted thoughts creeping in. He was labeling her and mind-reading and had no idea what was actually going on with her. He was also able to identify that he had been very passive in this situation. He hadn't expressed how her pattern of behavior was affecting him and had been letting his need for approval and his fear of confrontation get the best of him.

While working through Step 3, he was able to see the kind of relationship he hoped to have with her and how he could actually contribute to her being more successful in supporting the entire team. He was great

at creating systems and realized he could contribute something meaningful there.

Then we hit Step 4. Alan, like most people, got cold feet. His old
thought patterns started to emerge, and he said something that sounded
very Duty Paradigm to me: "I'm not her boss. She's mine! She should be
on top of her stuff, and I shouldn't have to take responsibility for her lack
of discipline."

After hearing this, I reminded him that while all of those thoughts
might have some merit, that's not the path he is on. He is not merely
trying to survive. He is trying to create change and learn what will work
better for him. I asked him to pretend that he was already fully in the
Integrity Paradigm and to imagine how he would shift his approach here.
He thought a while and responded that he would probably be most con-
cerned about the health of the team and about everyone's success and
learning from this challenge. He also acknowledged that he didn't know
what was really going on with his supervisor, and he would need to start
Step 4 by getting more perspective from her. He would also share more
openly about how this has been affecting him and let her know that he
really wanted to help her find a solution.

2. **How could I face my fear head on, stand in my power, and
    move this situation toward my ideal future vision?**

We need to remember that we are not the weak people our ego has
convinced us we are. And the world is not as threatening as the matrix
would have us believe. When you've done the work of the first three
steps, you can be assured that you are making choices that are clearer,
more real, more grounded in truth, and more likely to net positive
results. So, stand in your power. Remember all the great successes you've
had and the great things you've done in your life. Tap into your vision
for this situation that you started to form in Step 3 and picture what
steps you need to take to start to make real progress. Have confidence.
You are fully capable of influencing the details of your life to move
toward that vision.

COACHING ILLUSTRATION

Alan knew immediately that he would have to speak up with his boss in a way he never had before. He had that sinking feeling I warned you about! He acknowledged that his fear of confrontation was rooted in being rejected or disliked and never being able to recover from it. I asked him how likely it would be for his supervisor to respond to his vulnerability and honesty with dislike or even rude behavior. He said he had no reason to think that she would.

It was all old ego stuff. We revisited his vision for the situation, which included his vision for himself and the full team. He said he was committed to telling her how her past actions were affecting him, and he would express that he wanted to better understand her situation and find a way through it. He would listen to what was going on with her and look for opportunities to help identify an organizational system or communication process that could work better for them. He would also suggest that the full team talk together about how they could all help one another more with accountability and follow-through. He also would recommend that they create a charter for the team—around supporting one another, responding to requests in a timely way, etc.—based on what came up in the team conversation.

3. Looking back at my thoughts in Step 2, what opportunities are there for me to take actions that address my responsibility for this situation?

When we go through the questions in Step 2, we identify the approach we've been using that hasn't worked and think about better approaches that have worked in the past. We initially tend to answer with vague, high-level approaches such as "Take more action earlier" or "Speak up earlier when I'm unhappy."

That's great, but we want to build on that with some detail here in Step 4. Think about how that better approach could be applied here comprehensively. Challenge yourself to not only look at behavior moving forward, but also openly take responsibility for the past approach that didn't work. As you reflect on the better approach you could have used, think about all the dynamics at play in your Key Moment and really push yourself to take more responsibility for using a better approach in the numerous dynamics or elements of the situation.

COACHING ILLUSTRATION

In Step 2, Alan had identified that the approach he was using that didn't work was to avoid confrontation and to put more responsibility for his success on his supervisor, instead of taking full responsibility himself. He knew that in past situations at work when he wasn't getting support or resources he needed, if he spoke up early and brought possible solutions or ideas, it always turned out well.

When I pushed him to apply that approach more comprehensively in this situation, he said he not only wanted to take responsibility for his own work results and getting what he needed, but he also wanted to find a long-term solution for his supervisor as well as his entire team.

Building on his vision in the last coaching question, Alan said he wanted to actually volunteer to do the legwork of researching communication and collaboration resources and systems used on other teams in the company. He also wanted to tell his supervisor that he had been avoiding talking to her about this and that he would commit to avoid doing that in the future, asking her permission to do that. That would make him more likely to be accountable to himself and willing to face confrontation in the future when challenges arose.

4. Apply the Integrity Litmus Test: Will my planned actions create a win-win-win (a win for me, a win for others involved, and a win for our environment)?

It's very common for a little self-doubt to creep in here, and we can even talk ourselves out of some of the actions we've decided to take, or we can delay them with no real plan for when or how we want to take action. It's OK. You're fighting deeply ingrained thought and behavior patterns, remember? Give yourself a break! Make a solid plan and then run it through the litmus test so you can be fully confident that all the actions you've committed to take will net positive results for you in the long run.

Luckily, it's quite simple: win-win-win! Ask yourself: "Does each action create a win for me, others involved, and our environment? Am I positively contributing in every way I can, without overthinking it?"

Don't get into an ego-based thought pattern of worrying how it will turn out. That is a sure-fire opening for the matrix to step in and knock you sideways. Just run the test and trust that this system has been working for you and others throughout time. Win-win-win—sometimes the most profound lessons are the simplest.

COACHING ILLUSTRATION

Alan listed out the steps he was going to take and ran the litmus test on each one. He acknowledged that he was creating a win for himself for sure, and also for his colleagues and supervisor, and he was definitely creating a win for the environment, which in this case was his company and team. He also said he needed more information from his supervisor and his teammates to be able to really figure out what a win would be for them. He was assuming that they were also struggling with their supervisor not remembering things, but he wasn't sure this was true for everyone. Perhaps other issues would surface when he started the conversation. So his litmus test had a bit of a footnote. He said he wanted to commit to adapting his plan based on information he got along the way and asking others for their ideas on what a win would look like for the whole team. Perhaps the win would be a change or idea that could benefit the entire company.

> 5. After I've taken action: What aspect of my higher self (purpose, values, and/or principles) helped me to make the right move? What does this new approach I've taken tell me about what's really important to me?

I was tempted to make this its own step in the Adversity Cycle! We've discussed how the purpose of the Adversity Cycle is to help us learn, level up, and experience the next level of joy and fulfillment in our lives. The most powerful question in your learning and growth is right here in this final self-coaching question. After you implement the moves you've decided to take, reflect on this question and really cement the learning and growth you are gaining.

Then ask yourself: "How did I do it? How did I have the courage to take these steps? How did I have the wisdom to choose these new approaches? How did I find the discipline and commitment to take new, often more difficult actions in the face of adversity?" Simply put: "What part of my higher self fueled this transformation, and what does that tell me about its importance in my life?"

It may be a principle, like authenticity. Ask yourself: "If I was able to open up and become really vulnerable with someone about an insecurity I was experiencing in our relationship, and my principle of living with authenticity fueled my ability to do this, what have I learned about how to use this principle and how important it is? What transformed as a result of me living by this principle?"

And finally, ask yourself: "If I look at how I'm feeling about my integrity moves and the impact they've had on me internally, as well as my external environment, what have I really learned about what's *most* important to me? What's important to me in these kinds of situations, in relationships, in my work, and in my life? If I'm feeling proud, what am I really proud of, and how can I do more of that? If I'm feeling elated, what is really at the core of that? And how can I create more of that in my life? And if I'm feeling relieved, what am I relieved from, and how can I relieve myself from more of that negativity in my life?"

Listen to your heart. It knows. Your higher self speaks to you through your heart, not your head. These questions allow your higher self to tell you who you are meant to be and how you are meant to live. Listen carefully.

COACHING ILLUSTRATION

In Step 3, Alan identified that a really important principle he lived by when his higher self was in charge was the principle of honesty and transparency. He saw way too many instances in his life when people held back information or didn't really say how they were feeling, and he saw how it destroyed their relationships and also their happiness at work. He always swore he would not fall into that trap, but instead would express himself with honesty when the situation was important. He also acknowledged that he had a vision for himself being a peer leader on his team and demonstrating to others how they could contribute to the culture of the team. He would be an example of someone who always finds the positive in all situations. So, as Alan reflected back on his choices for integrity moves—specifically his choice to be open with his supervisor about how he had been avoiding talking with her about this challenge, his feelings, and how her actions were affecting his work—he became really afraid she would take the conversation the wrong way and become defensive or feel attacked.

Alan leaned into his principle of honesty when things are important. He realized that, no matter what, he had to be more open about where he was coming from and say it as respectfully as possible, if he was really going to move toward his vision for who he wanted to be on this team. After their conversation, his supervisor told him how much his sharing had opened her eyes. She said, "I keep thinking about how I didn't realize how much my lack of organization was affecting you. I feel bad, but I also feel so relieved that you told me, and now I'm really motivated to find better ways of supporting you guys."

Alan reflected on the importance of honesty, but also on the importance of delivering honest feedback in a way that is compassionate and respectful. He reflected on how the situation was teaching him what was most important to him, and he realized that while workflow and support were initially what seemed important in that Key Moment, what he found he was most excited about was this new level of relationship he had with his supervisor, and what a cool person she was turning out to be! He really liked *liking* her!

Alan hadn't realized how important quality relationships were to him, and he was surprised at how relieved he felt to know he could tell his supervisor anything. He decided to place more value on similar relationships in the future and always try to be the kind of person that anyone could say anything to without him becoming defensive. He would, like his supervisor, thank them for their honesty, no matter what.

Lanterns for This Step: Strength and Self-Love

Resistance shows up in this step in the most insidious of ways. You've gotten so close to a major breakthrough, but then the matrix steps back in to hold you back and keep you in survival mode. I hear over and over again, "I just don't know if I can do this," or "It's not worth it."

Always remember that your joy is worth it. Living a life of joy is what you're meant for. Love yourself enough to make it happen. Find the strength to battle that "I don't know if I can do this" resistance. It's quite simple. Use what has given you strength in the past. Go ahead. Do it!

Self-love is also a major source of Lanterns here. When you face the sometimes scary actions you have determined you want to take, you have to value yourself and your happiness enough to take those steps, difficult as they are. Think of the times in your life that you've had the most ful-fillment and joy and tell yourself that you will do whatever it takes to give yourself more joy and less suffering and frustration.

I often picture myself as a child, and then think of myself as a parent to that child. I imagine the kind of life I want for that child. I know I am the person who can let that child down or do whatever it takes to bring that child joy. It's my choice. And I love myself enough to follow through on my integrity moves.

OFF-PATH: EXCUSES

Self-betrayal occurs whenever we choose an action—or inaction—that we know is not in our best interest and that violates our integrity. I can hear you now: "What? Who, me? Betray myself? No way!" Uh, yes, dar-lin', you do it every day. In little ways. Ways that don't make much of an impact on your life. And you easily justify those ways with excuses. Remember that time you threw something recyclable in the trash? Or you didn't call that person back when you said you would?

Excuses are telling you things like "It's not that important" or "I'm busy and have to prioritize my time." But those tiny justifications are the exact same ones that you use to stop yourself from being happier and acting from a place of doing the right thing. From throwing something recyclable in the trash to lying to your boss about something important—it's a slippery slope.

Former president of the American Psychological Association and Professor Emeritus at Stanford University Philip G. Zimbardo, PhD, conducted years of research explaining how and why people end up committing malevolent or heinous acts. His work shows that people who end up doing really heinous, horrific things actually took a very consistent path to get there. They started by justifying small, kinda yucky actions, and over time the path progressed, little by little. So here's a trick for you to avoid self-betrayal. Examine the excuses you are using to not take the integrity action step you've worked so hard to identify and see them as considerations, not excuses.

Reframe any excuse—such as "I'm busy, so I'm going to put this off until it's truly worth my time"—so it becomes "I'm busy, which might be a challenge to my ability to take this action, so I'm going to address that challenge by contacting this person to schedule a twenty-minute phone call within the next two weeks to be sure I make time for it."

Poof! Bye-bye excuse and justification! The path of self-betrayal is paved with excuses, and you just hacked the shit out of that by taking the excuses your ego is creating and then using them to your advantage!

Exploring a Different Path

We often know what we should do to improve our lives, ourselves, our health, and our relationships, but we don't do it. Instead we betray ourselves. Please understand that this is part of our nature as humans. It's been happening across all cultures throughout all of time. It's a result of both the way our brain functions and the conditioning and programming we receive as we grow up and acculturate to the world around us.

But that doesn't make it OK. You will always slide into justifications and excuses, because they have been programmed into you, and they are a major component of the matrix. You've been swimming in the matrix your whole life. However, in Step 4 you are giving yourself the opportunity to explore a different path—the path of learning and creating a better life and then seeing what happens.

The proof is in the pudding! Just experiment with this step. Take baby steps and watch what happens. How do you feel? How do others respond to you? Give yourself a lot of grace, and once you've decided what your integrity moves are, love yourself enough to act on them. And most importantly, remember that the Adversity Cycle is a *cycle*! Come back around when a similar Key Moment comes into your life, or a similar kind of adversity surfaces. This is your cue to use the cycle again and go deeper. Revisit the patterns of adversity and see what else you can find.

You are spending more time in creation mode, and that in and of itself will reap great rewards. You won't be great at this at first. In fact, I tell my clients not to try to do it perfectly. Just take some action. Think about the concepts. Play and experiment. You'll get better, it will get easier, and you'll be more motivated to go deeper when you see the rewards in your life.

You are now totally loaded up with the details of each step in the cycle. Congratulations! Now you're ready for the final section of this guidebook, which contains lessons from the path of personal transformation. In Part 3, you'll learn survival tips, tricks, and proven practices to stay engaged and thriving on this path, as well as some warning signs to watch for what will try to knock you off course.

PART 3

Living the Adversity Cycle

The Transformative Value of the Work

Now that you have practiced the skills involved in each step of the Adversity Cycle and are beginning to see the transformative value of the work, I need to admit something to you. Though the Adversity Cycle is a very effective tool for unlocking new levels of joy, it is more than just a tool. It's also a way of life. You likely picked up this book for some finite reason, like reducing the suffering in your life, or advancing your career, or improving relationships, or having more financial success. And all of those are great reasons to do this work! The skills and awareness you develop will absolutely bring those things into your life. But now, think about it . . . you can actually achieve anything you want. Why stop here?

Maybe when you started to see progress in the initial goal you had for this work, you realized you wanted something else, something bigger. Or perhaps you have bigger questions that you've only just begun to answer. Or it could be that you recognize all this potential and ability you never knew you had, and now you want to know what else is possible for you. Maybe, just maybe, you've gained an unexpected amount of value from your work with the Adversity Cycle, and it's started to change your entire state of being.

Changing your state of being is the actual goal. The purpose of personal transformation is not to achieve something new, better, or different in your life. That's a side effect. A great side effect, to be sure, and fully worthy of the work you've put into this! However, what this work is ultimately about is freeing you from the matrix of oppressive, disempowering beliefs you've been programmed to live under so you can find a new way of living that is sharply focused on your own learning and growth. When personal growth and creating a new world around you are your main focus, you will experience a state of being that is at peace and grounded in what really matters. And that, my friends, is a path that never ends. And since you're always on one path or the other—survival or personal growth—why not pick that one that serves you?

So, yes, I'm telling you that this Adversity Cycle work doesn't end. I designed it to be a constantly expanding tool in your life that you can use over and over to go deeper and deeper into your learnings. When you do this, you will find yourself experiencing more joy, fulfillment, and equanimity for the majority of your waking minutes. Instead of trying to avoid conflict or challenges, you'll find yourself watching for what life has to teach you and bring you next. If you stay on this path, you'll be living your life in a way that values you, your lifetime on this planet, and the lives of those around you.

Rather than being a one-and-done, the Adversity Cycle is the means to a bigger, more exciting path. It's meant to open the door to your own discoveries. It has already helped you break out of an old way of being and enter into a new way of being that is, frankly, way freaking better. So let yourself wander and follow the new interests that pop up and the new questions that surface. Trust yourself to continue on this path of exploration and enlightenment. Before you picked up this book, you were most likely living in a bit of a haze. And now, as the haze is lifting, you're likely to find yourself drawn to new people, new books, new classes, new paths, and new experiences. Trust your higher self to point you in the direction that is next for you in life. Fill your heart and be a spark of joy and support for others! As far as I know, we only have this one life, so why not make the most of it and let go of the disempowering crap that has held you back so you can truly shine?

The next three chapters come to you from my heart and are grounded in a massive amount of study, personal experience, and experiences with my clients and colleagues who have chosen to stay on this path. These are your launchpad chapters. I designed them to propel you into this work so you can more easily transcend your current reality and live a life of constant growth and fulfillment. Think of them as your best practices for living what you've learned in the Adversity Cycle. As you continue to level up, the work will become second nature. When that happens, you will start using these skills as a way of life—a better life.

Chapter 8

Watch Out for the Matrix!

The Matrix in Your Life

Way back in the early parts of this book, I told you about a fundamental, existential truth found throughout ancient literature and spiritual teachings, which is now echoed in modern neuroscience and psychology: There are really only two general approaches to living. These approaches will determine how you're going to live your life on a minute-by-minute, hour-by-hour, week-by-week, and annual basis. The path you take mirrors the state of mind you choose.

You can choose to stay in survival mode (Life 1.0), or you can advance to learning and creating and upgrading your operating system (Life 2.0). If you continue to use the skills and tools of the Adversity Cycle and allow them to lead you to other skills for living a great life, you will remain on the path of learning and creation, aka personal transformation. However, if you are not intentional about operating by the rules of Life 2.0, you will inevitably be downgraded to your old operating system and be back in Life 1.0, experiencing the same issues and problems you had before you began this work. And there's a very simple explanation for this: the matrix.

The matrix is a brilliant and tricky little devil. It even knows how to thwart the very work of beating it! Think of the matrix as any belief or resistance that tricks you into engaging in dysfunctional behavior. Remember, you want to see reality clearly and shift your choices to align with what will work in your life. The matrix is essentially an alternate version of reality that mirrors the way things actually work in the world, but—and here's the kicker—the matrix version of reality is actually full of deception. It represents everything you *think* is true about the way the universe works. But, as you have learned, nothing in the matrix is actually true, and all of those beliefs create resistance that holds you back along your path of personal growth and transformation.

One very common example of this that I have found in my own life is the matrix-belief that an immense amount of hard work and long hours will help ensure your success in any endeavor. In fact, I thought that if I worked harder than other people, it would ensure I would be more successful than them! So, when things got rough, I looked around and said, "I'll just be sure to work harder and everything will be OK." But that was a matrix belief. I unquestioningly accepted it as truth. Then I started noticing there were a lot of really successful people who had done great things and weren't gritting it out, working fifty, sixty, or seventy-hour weeks without vacations. So, it must be possible to achieve great things without an immense amount of grit, right? Yep. I had believed a lie that conflicted with the way the universe actually works.

I've studied lots of existential texts and spiritual teachings and have even experimented with them in my life, and I've since realized that my belief of gritting it out was complete bullshit. It had horrible, detrimental effects on my life and on the lives of those around me. I felt guilty when I took a break. And I expected a tremendous work ethic from my colleagues and felt that we would fail if they weren't giving it their all, every second. I sacrificed fun, rejuvenation, and happiness to work harder to try to ensure my success, ironically stripping away the joy I was working so hard to attain.

That is the matrix.

But when I questioned my belief, I felt very threatened. That is, my ego felt threatened. If working hard wouldn't ensure my success, what would? And if I let that go, what could I count on? So I had to get curious and read and talk and question, and experiment with new beliefs and approaches. In reality I just needed to be more aware and make better decisions and not work myself to death.

Feeling threatened when I challenged a core belief and guilty or afraid if I tried to deviate from it is a perfect example of the matrix at work. For years I clung to this belief that I and everyone else around me had to give our all, all day, every day. It was a core belief, something that I absolutely knew to be true. But the thing is, it wasn't true at all.

So how did I figure it out? By doing this work and using adversity to teach me. I got clarity on what was really important to me and started studying my life. The work helped me question and reflect on what was actually important to me. It shined a bright light on my faulty belief and showed me what wasn't working, along with what I really wanted, which led to me trying out new approaches. And most importantly, while I was doing this, I was observing how those choices were working for me. I was constantly checking in with myself and asking: "What am I learning?" And equally important, "What am I unlearning?" Because I stuck with it, the path of learning and creation allowed me to uncover those untruths lurking in the matrix so I could break free and find my truth.

Where the Matrix Lurks

However, as I said, this isn't a one-and-done. So when the challenges begin to pile up or big adversity comes my way, just like anyone else, I am lured back into those old matrix beliefs. Whenever my thoughts start reverting back to Life 1.0, I hear things like *Just work harder, Meg, and everything will be OK.* When this happens, I have to catch the matrix thinking in my head and say, *HELLZNO. I already called you on your shit, matrix, and this is not something I believe anymore.*

So, with this new level of adversity, I will not succumb to those old matrix beliefs that made me feel better and more in control—because they just don't work. Instead, I will go back to the Adversity Cycle and the lessons I've learned along the way, and I will continue down the path of success.

The matrix will always be there, whispering to me, whispering to you. As Dr. Morguelan outlines in the teachings of Energy for Success, the matrix has twists and turns and comes at you from many surprising directions. When you begin to master those twists and turns, you can much more easily win in life, living more of your waking hours as your higher self, on the path of learning and creation, experiencing peace, clarity, and brilliance instead of confusion, stress, and overwhelm. Here's a short list of where I've found the matrix lurking. In this list you will also learn how it subtly grabs us. This will arm you with another adversity hack so you can have the best chance of heading it off, or at least sidestepping around it whenever it starts to grab you.

Other People

First, the matrix is lurking in *so* much of what other people tell you, especially when times are hard. That's because they believe the matrix! Remember, we all do . . . until we don't. Most people haven't done this work, so they will continue to throw their matrix beliefs at you. As if it wasn't hard enough to battle your own habitual thoughts, right? They will reinforce your bullshit narrative—the ways of thinking that are antithetical to the path of personal transformation. You may hear things like "people never change" or "that dream you have for your life is probably not attainable" or "your happiness isn't that important; you should focus on following the rules and staying out of trouble." Whenever you hear things like this, know they are all bullshit matrix beliefs you uncover when you are on this path. But other people believe them with all their hearts. In most instances, they aren't trying to mislead you. They are trying to comfort you or help you to just fit in and not struggle. But they are telling you things that are only true in the matrix and the path of survival.

Your Subconscious

The matrix also lurks in your subconscious—you know, those old, deeply engrained, habitual thought pathways in your mind. However, as I progress on the path of transformation, I gain strength and clarity, so I see the matrix beliefs for what they are, and so will you. It's probably already happening for you, isn't it? Such a beautiful thing when it does! But it takes time to pull up all that old, crappy thinking and prove it wrong at deeper and deeper levels. Old thoughts creep back into our heads, especially when we're tired or facing a new level of adversity. Remember your skills in Step 1: You don't have to believe your thoughts. Most of them are just preprogrammed stuff from your time on the path of survival.

Your Ego

The matrix can always speak to you directly through your ego. Your ego is the matrix's gate into your thoughts. Whenever you feel threatened, unsafe, uncomfortable, or something important to you is threatened—watch out! That's when your ego pops up and becomes a megaphone for matrix thoughts. The goal is to know very quickly and accurately which voice is talking to you: your ego or your higher self. I've learned to listen to my higher self and placate my ego as I push it back into the backseat, gagged and blindfolded.

Attachments

It's vital to understand how the matrix has power over you, so you can see it as it's happening and call it out! Another way the matrix lures you back into survival and self-protection is through attachments. There are libraries of books written on attachments in spirituality and psychology, but here's my easy-to-understand CliffsNotes version.

As you've been living and experiencing the world, bad shit happened that caused you pain. Your mind worked hard to figure out the source of that pain and to develop a gazillion strategies to avoid and get out of that pain. These strategies evolved into beliefs about the world and the best way for you to interact with it. These beliefs led to attachments.

We attach to the things we think are going to help us avoid pain and suffering and experience more happiness. For example, I might have figured out in school that I can avoid being bullied if I get people to like me. Then I eventually became attached to people liking me. I *need* people to like me, because I think it's vital to my happiness. Another common attachment is to money or status. We are afraid of not having enough, or being trapped or limited in our choices, so we decide that money or power over others is necessary. And, eventually we become attached to money—we want more and more, and we believe that we can't be OK without it, but it doesn't actually ever bring us the joy we are seeking.

Like everything in the matrix, attachments are a trick. Those attachments end up thwarting our progression, because they are emotion-driven and survivalist and thus built on a foundation of misperception and even lies. They are almost always perceived as harmless and logical, and sometimes even good. For example, if I'm attached to being married to my husband, I would feel extremely threatened by anything I thought might lead to his leaving me. If I simply find joy in my marriage to my husband but am not attached to it, I don't feel like I need to be married to him to be OK or happy. I find joy in our relationship, but I know I'd be OK if the marriage ended.

You can be attached to anything. In this instance, the marriage becomes something else to you because of your attachment to it. It's not just having a relationship with someone who brings you joy, or someone who brings financial stability to your life. It becomes about your belief that you won't have joy or financial stability without it. And BAM—attachment.

Attachments then drain the love, opportunity, and growth out of the relationship or whatever it is you're attached to. It might be specific relationships, or kinds of interactions, or roles you play, or drugs or alcohol, or certain aspects of your lifestyle, or money, or something you perceive to keep you safe, make you liked, keep you happy, prove your worth, etc.

Attachments can be identified by asking yourself, "What do I believe I need to be OK? What am I terrified of losing?" The key word is *need*—it's a sign you're attached. It's all rooted in your fear of suffering, your fear that bad things that happened before are going to happen again, and you must avoid them at all cost. The matrix will use your attachments to sneak back in and cloud your ability to see reality.

If I were attached to my marriage, and my husband came home talking about a new female friend that he had a great time with, that might trigger a fear that he was going to leave me for that friend, which would cause me to interpret reality with personalization or mind-reading distortions like "He's going to end up falling in love with her" or "Why doesn't he talk about me that way? Aren't I as funny as she is?" And just like that, I'm no longer hearing about his good time and celebrating that with him. I'm experiencing irrational fear because of my attachment. Someone who doesn't have that attachment would not experience the situation like that at all, right? That's why, during Step 1, we try to identify the irrational fears that are triggering our distorted thinking and shaping our thoughts and actions.

How to Know When the Matrix Has You by the Balls

As you continue down this path, the matrix will continually try to trick you. It doesn't want you to progress; it only wants you to stay comfortable in the status quo, powerless to change your life. It's helpful to think of the matrix as a dense but invisible web of lies wrapped around your thinking. Like someone suffering with schizophrenia who believes that everyone is trying to poison them, you've unquestioningly accepted this web of lies as completely true. Most of the matrix beliefs you hold were programmed into you by your family and the teachers in your life, as it was to them by their families and teachers—so much so that the matrix has become invisible to us.

The Top Ten Signs You're Off-path

Tripping up is part of the work. It's how we learn and strengthen our resolve. I'm going to share a matrix hack with you, what I like to call The Top Ten Signs You're Off-path. When you find yourself engaging in these thoughts or actions, you're so Off-path that you're actually mired down in the matrix. Those are the moments when the matrix has you by the balls. The telltale signs are as follows:

1. Having regret or resentment

2. Ignoring complexity/clinging to being right

3. Engaging in a useless, desperate search for happiness

4. Believing you are who you are and cannot change

5. Thinking you're done doing the work of personal growth, learning, or transformation

6. Dealing in the economy of self-pity, judgement, and blame

7. Getting sucked into the vortex of judging those on the path of survival

8. Needing the negative

9. Believing you don't have time or that you should use your time for "more important" things

10. Experiencing anxiety and overwhelm

HAVING REGRET OR RESENTMENT

Your thoughts—the narrative you're spinning about all the circumstances in your life—are consistent with past thoughts, beliefs, and actions that have caused you regret or resentment. For example, I think I've overcome big hurdles doing this work. I've improved my relationship with my husband tremendously by no longer judging him and blaming him. Even then, some resentment creeps in and I start to think, *He's not doing as much as I am,* or *He's being lazy today.* That's the exact thinking that messed up my relationship with him and resulted in a hundred Key Moments in our relationship, so I need to put that in check. When the old narrative starts to creep back in, just see the thoughts for what they are: complete and utter bullshit. Then step around them and look for the complexity and opportunity in the Key Moment. When our brains put up blinders and we start to see things as black and white, feeling like a victim in our lives, we are in the foggy veil of the matrix.

IGNORING COMPLEXITY/CLINGING TO BEING RIGHT

If you acknowledge that you want to progress from your current level of awareness and understanding, you are admitting that you have even more potential. However, you lack a clear understanding of that new level of potential and what it will look like, or you would already be there.

Think about it—let's say ignorance comes from resistance to truths. Truths like:

- I can handle this.

- I created this Key Moment.

- This person who's hurting me loves me, and I love them.

- It's not as simple as people behaving badly toward me. Rather, they are acting out of pain.

- I participated in what has brought them pain.

- These are old patterns for both of us.

- This situation is being worsened by a lack of sleep and a tight deadline.

We resist those truths for more convenient, ego-based beliefs like, "I'm right, and she is wrong," or "She is hurting me because she's a bad person." That's not Truth; that's ignorance. The crux of our progression is to fight this ignorance by letting go of our resistance to truth.

Nice thought, right? But how do we do that? I'm glad you asked. All you need to do is accept that you aren't seeing the full picture of anything, ever. Then admit that there is an opportunity you're not seeing yet and that you haven't realized your potential. Is that it? Yep, and that shit will *work*, y'all! Try it!

I question every thought that comes into my head now, not out of cynicism but rather a desire to see the world in a more complete, rational, complex, and constructive manner. I embrace the fact that every opinion that pops into my brain is flawed and likely fundamentally bullshit. When I lean into that perspective, I find the magic and open up to the real Truth.

I use the Adversity Cycle laid out in this book to uncover amazing truths. I find that I'm capable in ways I never would have thought and see myself progress in ways I didn't even know were possible. But I have to stop resisting the truth and resisting higher levels of consciousness. I work to pull that ignorance up out of my subconscious. Remember, we created those beliefs to avoid trauma and pain, and those beliefs settled into our subconscious. They drive our behavior from there, below the surface. We access a new level of understanding when we let go of an ignorant belief and stop resisting reality and truth. That new understanding brings us to a higher level of consciousness. Pretty. Freaking. Badass. Right?

ENGAGING IN A USELESS, DESPERATE SEARCH FOR HAPPINESS

I know we've talked about this. But you're gonna do it, so let's revisit it for a second. Happiness is an emotion and, by nature, fleeting. There's nothing wrong with it, but it comes and goes, and you don't have much control over it. Joy, on the other hand, is a state of being. It comes from having experiences that are fulfilling and engaging in activities and ways of being that are consistent with what you're wired to do and be. If a series of actions, or type of behavior, results in an undesirable state of being (e.g., low-energy, depressed, resentful, burdened) then it's time to reexamine it and try something else. If that new action, belief, or behavior results in joy, then do more of that. It's that simple.

Happiness is great, but all it means is that you shot some dopamine into your brain. Being a happiness junkie is just like being addicted to drugs. Judging the quality of your life by the amount of time you spend in happiness is foolish. Again, there's nothing wrong with happiness. It's just not the goal. If you make it the goal, you're submitting to the matrix.

Happiness also doesn't help you learn and progress in life. Its value is limited. Don't let yourself be tricked into making happiness your gauge of success. What a brilliant distraction of the matrix—having you constantly seeking out something that is fleeting and meaningless!

BELIEVING YOU ARE WHO YOU ARE AND CANNOT CHANGE

That's just not true. Humans can continue to grow up, level up, and progress. In fact, we're meant to do so, and we tend to become mentally unhealthy and dysfunctional when we stop. Yet our modern culture often perpetuates this notion that when you're an adult, you can stop growing. What a bunch of crap! You are an evolving being. You are not the same person you were even two years ago. So stop believing that you are.

Most of what we consider to be our personality is in a state of constant evolution. We can develop and shift it. Your higher self is how you were wired by nature. That won't change, and it's usually very basic and simple. Personality, on the other hand, is complex and involves a ton of factors. My best advice here is that when you make reference to yourself (out loud, in conversation, or even just in your head), refer to personal traits, characteristics, and beliefs in the past tense. Instead of saying, "I don't like risks," say, "I have avoided risks in the past." I'm asking you to do this because your likes and wants are always evolving and changing. When you state a former belief or trait about yourself as constant, you cage yourself in your past. Please stop doing that and free yourself instead!

THINKING YOU'RE DONE DOING THE WORK OF PERSONAL GROWTH, LEARNING, OR TRANSFORMATION

The thing is, I still haven't met anyone who's arrived. If you have any emotion or experience that you perceive as negative and don't want it in your life, you have work to do. I have yet to meet someone who is fully in harmony with the world around them at every given moment and who lives a life where every single action they take is one of integrity and promotes more joy in their life and the lives of others. Therefore, if the silly matrix tries to trick you into believing you're done with this work, see it for the matrix lie it really is. (Having said that, if you do arrive, call me! I want to know how you did it, and we'll shout it from the mountain tops together!)

DEALING IN THE ECONOMY OF SELF-PITY, JUDGEMENT, AND BLAME

Here's the sad truth: As soon as you start reinforcing other people's ego-based narratives, you subtly reinforce the influence of your own ego over your thinking. It's *soooo* tempting! You know what I'm talking about: that friend who complains about her husband not doing enough around the house; that colleague who starts complaining about a difficult personality you both have to work with; that little voice in your own head that tells you that people are stupid and harmful.

When people want you to engage in their narrative of bullshit, you perpetuate the bullshit not only for them but also for yourself. Just *stop*. However, I must warn you, empowering yourself will trigger other people. When this happens, just show them some compassion and remember your own struggles. And if they are open to it, share something with them that might help them.

I've made a commitment not to disempower people by reinforcing their narratives that come from a place of survival and ego and that do not serve them. Instead, I show empathy and care. I love them, so I refuse to reinforce their narratives by agreeing with their suppositions. It's uncomfortable, because as a society we've kind of made a pact to agree with each other's bullshit, especially when we are in pain.

I've worked hard not to do this, while still showing love and empathy, and sometimes that really pisses people off. For example, when my friend complains about her terrible boss and how there's no pleasing him, I could agree with her, but I don't. Instead, I empathize and say I've felt stuck in dealings with difficult personalities, too, but I don't agree that it's an impossible situation. Then she tries to convince me that it's impossible, and I don't agree. And man, that really pisses people off sometimes! But guess what? They stop coming to me with their bullshit unless they actually want to explore it from a different perspective. And you know what? That's just fine with me!

GETTING SUCKED INTO THE VORTEX OF JUDGING THOSE ON THE PATH OF SURVIVAL

I see this over and over with my clients, and I've fallen into this trap as well. We do this incredible work to pull ourselves out of old distorted narratives; we take responsibility for our lives, and we live from a higher-self, an integrity driven place, and we see so clearly when other people are not doing these things.

But here's the deal: It's a dangerous, slippery slope to assume you know the minds of others and even more dangerous to place judgement on them. So what if they are using a thought distortion? They are human and have a human brain operating system 1.0, just like you. So what if they're not seeing how they caused the crap they are complaining about? You do it, too!

The key here is to remember that there isn't one dysfunctional or unattractive human behavior that you yourself have not fallen prey to, likely in the recent past. Have grace. Remember that you were just swimming in that dirty pond of self-deception and self-betrayal, and you still get sucked back in periodically by the matrix. You are no better; you are no different.

If you want to help, give them this book. Give them encouragement. Give them whatever they might need to be supported in a different direction. Judging and blaming them is a trap. Don't get sucked into the distorted narrative that you are better than anyone else. It's all ego. It's all bullshit. Stay strong and stay loving, and you'll do just fine.

When confronted with other people's shit, which you will be, just be your higher self. Be an example of courage, empathy, strength, and kindness. That will change the world and keep you on the path of personal transformation.

NEEDING THE NEGATIVE

This need is basically an addiction to suffering. Wait, what? Why would anyone be addicted to suffering? Bear with me here. Pain is for learning. Think of it as the universe telling you that your approach isn't working. Learning pains will always come your way. It's part of the existential reality of the human condition. However, suffering is different. Suffering is actually clinging to your pain. Suffering is wholly unnecessary and in fact, is a choice.

Sometimes we overidentify with our pain and think it's part of who we are. We don't know who we would be without it, and that scares us.

We perpetuate the same patterns that bring us pain, dwell on our pain, think about it, and talk about it endlessly in order to have something to identify with. We can lose track of who we are without something to complain about.

Have you ever talked with someone and realized that most of what they have said is complaining? Do you think that might be you? This is someone who has fallen into the trap of being addicted to pain. Another way of saying this is that they believe they *are* their pain, and they believe their pain is something meaningful because it gives them purpose. Their addiction to the pain gives them a sense of purpose and identity, so they keep it in their life.

If you find yourself at a crossroads in life, with the opportunity to walk away from something that has caused you a lot of pain, and you're having second thoughts, ask yourself if you feel more comfortable (more like yourself) when you have that pain. Ask yourself if you might actually be afraid of losing it. It sounds crazy, but almost all of us have slipped into this at some point in our lives. It's a natural response to living in the matrix.

BELIEVING YOU DON'T HAVE TIME OR THAT YOU SHOULD USE YOUR TIME FOR "MORE IMPORTANT" THINGS

This is such a popular matrix deception these days! It drives me crazy as a coach. Are you freaking kidding me? Let's say I have a huge amount of work ahead of me in the next week, and I know I'll barely be able to get it all done, and I don't have a spare minute. And then, I get sick, or my kid gets sick, or a friend or family member has a crisis and needs me. I make time. And things end up OK.

The matrix wants you to believe that all the stuff you currently think is priority is actually priority. But maybe a bunch of that stuff is not priority, and maybe it isn't bringing you the value you think it is! Time is an illusion. Priority is everything. Don't you think the path of survival is paved with the stuff you've already been doing and prioritizing? Isn't your life and what's important to you worth some time? Plus, thinking differently doesn't take that much time.

I do the reflections of the Adversity Cycle in the shower, at stoplights, or while folding laundry. My friend, please hear this: You have time to change your life. Anything else is a matrix lie. So, when you find yourself sliding back into old ways of spending your time and old priorities creep back in, it's time for a serious reboot.

The matrix will always give you plenty of reasons to not value your higher self enough to cultivate your life intentionally. It will always give you plenty of reasons to take shortcuts. But you do value yourself. You want a better life, or you would not have made it this far in the work. The matrix, which is all around you, and also expressed in the words and ideas of others around you all the time, will always try to suck you back in. If your personal transformation is not a priority, the backslide of the matrix will suck you in. I hate that this is true, but it's been proven time and again. Honor yourself with a daily commitment to the path of growth and creation and finding new levels of joy.

EXPERIENCING ANXIETY AND OVERWHELM

If you are experiencing sharp anxiety or feelings of being overwhelmed, the matrix has definitely crept in there and grabbed you by the balls. This is a big one—and a really, really common one. Anxiety is no more real than any other daydream or matrix idea, but people around you will always tell you otherwise. This is a slippery one! But let's disprove the trick of anxiety and overwhelm right now!

Consider this: Several years ago there were activities, situations, or tasks that overwhelmed you or created anxiety within you that no longer have that hold on you. Also, things that might overwhelm someone else may not overwhelm you and vice versa. Therefore, it's completely possible for you to face the challenges you know lie ahead, or the amount of tasks on your plate, and feel *no* anxiety. You are creating this anxiety by holding on to the old, very subtle, matrix-based beliefs.

I can honestly say that I'm more productive than I've ever been in my life. My days are incredibly full, and I'm accomplishing an amazing amount of work on a daily and weekly basis, and I experience zero anxiety or feelings of being overwhelmed. Realizing that I was creating this illusion of anxiety and overcoming it has created such a profound sense of relief that it's hard to put into words. This was a *huge* matrix lie that took me a year to unlearn and disbelieve.

What if you believed you were fully capable of doing everything ahead of you with ease and grace? What if you decided that you wanted to do it all with a sense of peace instead of angst, frustration, or impatience? What if you believed you would get everything done you needed to do, and everything would be just fine? In his book *The Power of Now*,[1] Eckhart Tolle very eloquently lays out a profound teaching that illustrates the nature of this lie. He teaches that if you are truly living in the present moment, there is no anxiety; there are no problems. There is just your current experience.

However, we tend to project ourselves forward into the future and create ideas and beliefs about how the future will be, based on our past experience. Or not even on past experience, but on how we choose to remember past experiences and what meaning we place on them. But if you are living in the NOW and not projecting into the future, there is no anxiety. You might have stuff to do today, but there is absolutely no need to create a negative projection about the future and your experience of the things you anticipate you will be doing.

You might have heard the old adage "People who live in the future are anxious, and people who live in the past are depressed." If I'm focused on the now, on what I want to do, and on the infinite opportunities I have each day, I have no reason to experience either anxiety or depression.

What if you remembered your past experiences through a lens of all the great things you've done, how well you've handled life, and how any surprises you found supported you and inspired you? As Dr. B says, "If you remembered every victory in your life rather than every failure, imagine what your life would be like." Would you have anxiety about the future? Or would you see yourself as competent and capable, growing and learning and receiving support from others around you whenever you need or want it?

Unfortunately, that's not how most of us chose to view the past. We focus on the negative, the times when we felt inept. But what if that was

---

1   Eckhart Tolle, *The Power of Now: A Guide to Spiritual Enlightenment* (Novato, CA: New World Library, 1999).

all *thought distortion* and not real? If you've learned the skills of Step 1, you know that your perception is not reality, even in the moment. So why would your memory be any more real, rational, or true?

It all boils down to choice. You can choose to paint a picture of your life in the past, present, or future. If you simply live in the now you don't need to place a bunch of distorted meaning on what you are seeing and experiencing; if you disidentify with your constant chatter of thoughts coursing through your mind, then you will be free from the grips of the matrix when it tries to suck you in. This, my friends, is a worthy endeavor. So nice try, matrix, but we have no need for anxiety and overwhelm.

Step-by-Step

Dang, that's a lot of crap to overcome and navigate around, right? I wanted to lay this out for you as clearly as I could to give you the concrete tips and strategies that will allow you to smoothly progress through the foggy haze of the matrix and discover new ways of living that bring you so much more joy. It's not a smooth or clear path. (Thus, the Lanterns!) The only way to break out of the matrix is to, step-by-step, one foot in front of the other, prove to yourself that there is a different way of being that is more true and more joyful. If you find that you are reliving old patterns, or just not as joyful as you want to be, or you have a *really big* Key Moment, come back to this chapter and skim through it again. I guarantee you will find a path-saving nugget to guide you out of the matrix and into the light so you can see the bullshit for what it really is and step around it.

Chapter 9

Top Ten Proven Strategies to Keep Moving on the Path of Transformation

To be totally blunt, I worked my ass off on this book for one reason: my higher self made me. Hah! OK, that's only half true. Really, here it is: My personal purpose is to help you. I only want one thing for you, and I've developed a powerful tool to help you get it. I want you to realize what a true badass you really are so you can free yourself from suffering permanently.

But this path gets pretty darn hairy! Having been traveling it and diligently helping others get started down it for many years, I know that there will always be times when we get knocked off the path and have to put ourselves back on it.

No one can do this work for you. It's about your discipline and commitment. But I'm here to help you navigate some of the challenges, which is why in this chapter you will learn the top ten proven tricks and tips to stay on the path effortlessly!

Come back to these whenever you're back in the dark and living the old life. Pick a couple to commit yourself to and use them to guide yourself back to this incredible path of personal learning and fulfillment. You won't need these right away, but you will eventually. Hang on to this book, keep coming back to this chapter, and use these tips whenever you need to! Apply whatever feels useful at the time. It could be Tips 3 and

7 one month and something completely different the next. Eventually these behaviors will become habitual, making this work almost effortless!

The top ten strategies are as follows:

1. Laugh at yourself.

2. Use the Lanterns.

3. Meditate.

4. Practice gratitude regularly.

5. Renew and rejuvenate yourself.

6. Get a coach.

7. Protect yourself from what doesn't give you fuel and energy.

8. Celebrate victories and wins.

9. Feed your soul.

10. Embrace challenge.

Strategy 1: Laugh at Yourself

You gotta have fun. But first you need to get out of your own frigging way! Did you know you're causing *all* of your own suffering? Think about that for a second. I mean, that's actually pretty hilarious, right? You don't want to suffer, yet you're causing your suffering?

OK, so maybe you're not laughing yet. That's OK. Keep practicing. A sense of humor will get you through this work with grace, so fake it until you make it. Next time you fall or cheat on your diet or forget to pick up your kid at school, try laughing at yourself instead of making yourself feel bad by perpetuating your own suffering with those old paradigms of duty, fear, integrity, and achievement. Next time you reflect and realize how much you totally screwed up a situation, or you let stress get the best of you and let your ego take over, observe your behavior with humor! Know that you are doing this because you are operating with a human brain, and you are in a constant, evolving process of raising your awareness and level of functioning. Setbacks can actually be a funny reminder of your areas for continued growth.

The universe is sending you these little signals of pain for your own learning, and instead of learning you're completely losing it and letting a little pain knock you on your ass! What a silly, silly human condition! Laughing when you experience pain reclaims your power, because you don't let the pain consume you. The laughter diffuses the pain and stops suffering right in its tracks. And the matrix hates it when you figure that out, because it can no longer control you.

I have friends who are also doing this work, and I joke repeatedly about how whatever lesson I'm learning at the moment seems so basic after I have that aha moment. I think it's hilarious to be in my forties and have somehow forgotten how to speak up for myself, how to know what brings me joy, how to be unapologetic about my boundaries, how all those little things that I used to think were so important are not important at all. For example, I can laugh when someone rear-ends me, or I fall while skiing, or my kid has a tantrum in public. Because I know these are all small moments for learning and growth, and they don't really matter, and actually they are quite comical!

So laugh at yourself every day. That will show the matrix (and your creepy little ego) that *you* are in control of your mind and your approach to life. You know who you are and what is important. Laugh and show the matrix who's boss. That, my friends, is power.

Strategy 2: Use the Lanterns

Remember to use the Lanterns explained in each stage of the process in Part 2. Darkness will come and confuse you again. You're living in a world full of the matrix. You're surrounded by people living in the matrix and believing it's real. They are suffering, and what does misery love? Yes, company.

The pull of the matrix will always suck you away from this work. Remember, the matrix doesn't want you to progress and realize your potential. And it's so wired into you, and into those around you, that it will always find subtle ways to slip back into your thinking and convince you that this work is not that important or that all those dreams you had are not that important.

When you know you are struggling and feeling resistance to the work at any point in your life, use the Step 1 Lanterns and ask yourself, "What if I just stayed really curious? What if I approach today with more intention and discernment?" The work of mastering the distinctions of the Lanterns along the path is incredibly rewarding and actually downright magical. It will keep you feeling invincible. The matrix will come, and challenges will come, but you will continue to gain more awareness and proficiency in stepping around them—and more importantly, learning from them.

Strategy 3: Meditate

It's like a cleaning cycle for your brain! Come on, everyone's doing it! I'm only half kidding. Yes, meditation. Ugh. I know, I hated it too. But I didn't really understand what it was. I encourage you to visit YouTube for a huge variety of guided meditations. Make it easy on yourself. If you start to look around and see what *really* successful people are doing that they say fuels them, well, they are freaking meditating! There are tons of ways to meditate, and you can get a lot of free and affordable help to build some skill in this. I've learned that we are wired for this—it's like medicine for your brain, cleaning away the damaging, toxic pathways of thought that are holding you back.

Just ten minutes every other day can work wonders. Meditation is a powerful practice for **going beyond habitual, conditioned thought patterns into a state of expanded awareness.** It unlocks those aha moments and helps us more easily identify and step around old conditioning and ego-based thinking. Through mediation we open ourselves to new insights, intuition, and ideas. Even if all you're doing is noticing the mind jumping about—doing that crazy, monkey-brain thing—you're meditating. If your mind quiets as a result of being observed (which it often does), that's wonderful. But whether it does or not is of no consequence. Just watching your thoughts as an observer allows you to be in the moment and not attached to your mind. That's it.

Meditating regularly will bring you *huge* rewards far greater than the time investment you spend doing it. You've probably experienced some frustration and difficulty with the skills involved in each step of the Adversity Cycle. It seems too hard, or frustrating, or unclear, depending on the Key Moment or adversity you are facing. Meditation makes this work easy. It's that simple. It makes it easy for you to see your shit, embrace better approaches to life, step around your fears, and realize what is most important to you.

But really, why meditate? It feels boring and pointless to most people, so if you're like me, you need some concrete reasons to try it out. I encourage everyone to research it a bit and see what science has found as the physical and psychological benefits of meditation. In his book *The Science of Enlightenment*,[1] Shinzen Young lists these key benefits of meditation, among others:

- **The ability to experience unavoidable pain with less suffering**

- **An increased ability to appreciate small pleasures**

- **Understanding who you really are at the deepest level**

- **Improved ability to change behavior**

---

1   Shinzen Young, *The Science of Enlightenment: How Meditation Works* (Boulder, CO: Sounds True, 2016).

- Finding within yourself the authentic desire to contribute to the happiness of others and to love more fully

Sounds pretty good to me for a practice that can take as little as twenty minutes every other day. And, if you're like me and really struggle to sit quietly for twenty minutes or so, I strongly encourage you to do guided visualizations. *Energy for Success* on YouTube offers tons of them. Guided visualizations have allowed me to finally be quite content with that daily practice of sitting down and cleaning out my brain, and the impact is every bit as effective as more traditional forms of meditation.

Strategy 4: Practice Gratitude Regularly

Be grateful for what your life has brought you. You will begin to notice that the universe has your back. Be grateful for that opportunity at work that came out of nowhere! Be grateful for that act of kindness from a good friend or that total stranger! The final chapter of this book will discuss these little magical manifestations I like to call the Ripple Effect. For now, I invite you to start a practice of gratitude.

Different events in our lives, even adversity, bring us the opportunity to uncover something we are really grateful for that we might have taken for granted—like when the electricity goes out in your home. Struggle can also show us how grateful we can be for the basics like a roof over our heads; warm, running water; or safety.

There are libraries of books and articles written on gratitude, its power in your life, and how to let it guide you. By incorporating gratitude practices into our days, we're essentially taking time for the path of learning and creation—just by the act of connecting with what we are thankful for and want more of in our lives.

You can take a structured approach by writing in a daily gratitude journal or making a gratitude list each night. Conversely, you can take an unstructured approach and just be very mindful each day about recognizing what you are grateful for and occasionally meditating on gratitude or having a spontaneous discussion at the dinner table about what everyone is grateful for. Any time you spend connecting to what you actually care about and appreciate is time well spent, because you'll be able to know what your higher self really wants. In turn, this will help you choose more integrity moves that bring you even more of it!

Nothing will help you learn more about what is important to you than gratitude. What are you thankful for? How did it come to be? Was it a serendipitous gift from the universe? Or did you create it? *Both* are huge wins and things to be celebrated. The clearer you are about what you are grateful for, the more of it you will bring into your life.

Strategy 5: Renew and Rejuvenate Yourself

I'm talking real renewal and rejuvenation here, not numbing, escape, or indulgence in attachments. Not that there is anything fundamentally wrong with a little escape or numbing—it just does nothing for your progress in this work of creating a better life for yourself. Let's be clear: Rejuvenation is different and is defined as "the action or process of making someone or something look or feel better, younger, or more vital." It's not escaping from adversity only to come back with the same attitude, energy level, and crappy approach. Rejuvenation is an activity that actually makes you feel healthier, more energized, and more vital, with renewed vigor and vibrancy for the struggles ahead. If your cup isn't full, how can you overflow to help others? Neuroscience tells us that when our brains are stressed, our IQ drops, our emotions more easily overwhelm us and influence us negatively, and we become very self-focused and closed-minded. If you are operating from a place of depletion and overwhelm, you will have less energy and less ability to support other people. And, let's face it, we all get a little banged up throughout our days and weeks.

As you do this work, you will begin to feel less and less like you are getting banged up! You will be less easily triggered and knocked sideways by the events of your day. However, you are still functioning with a human brain that is wired for emotion and self-protection, so take care of yourself. I always found "self-care" to be a hollow and silly concept; therefore, I didn't do it. Big mistake. I just didn't understand what people meant.

Rejuvenation is different. It's the restoration of youthful vigor, and who couldn't use some of that? I find that my clients get it when I ask them to identify two or three activities that leave them feeling better afterward, during which they forget who they are, what work they have to do, and what stresses them. They just *are*. Like flow! The key is that you feel better *afterward*. I find a glass of wine can be nice, but it doesn't make me feel better after it wears off or even the next day.

On the other hand, rejuvenating activities, such as exercise, yoga, massage, indulging in a sport or hobby, playing with a child, singing, reading a great book, and meditation, give you energy and vigor for life. Be aware that what rejuvenates one person might not rejuvenate another. Personally, I've found some of the activities that rejuvenate me the most have been activities that I've resisted, such as yoga or the physical practices I've learned. My mind tells me they are a waste of time, but I can't deny how much more energy, strength, and peace I have after I do them. We are all really different, so you'll just have to pay attention to how you feel after different activities to become more aware of what's actually rejuvenating for you. If you don't know what rejuvenates you, start experimenting and find some activities that nourish you. They are your lifeline.

Strategy 6: Get a Coach

Over and over again, I see people commit to improving their emotional intelligence, wanting to level up, make better decisions, and have less stress. And then when given the tool and the support, they resist. They don't prioritize the work, or they don't follow through. I've been there. We all have. We also get a little stuck sometimes when a Key Moment overwhelms us and we can't see how to apply the concepts.

For example, you've been using the tool just fine on Key Moments, and then a *huge* adversity hits—a Key Moment to end all Key Moments (like divorce or the loss of a loved one)—and everything you've figured out through your use of this tool seems as though it doesn't apply to this big Key Moment. However, this is when you know a big lesson is coming—and this next breakthrough will be huge and awesome!

Anticipate and accept your resistance, knowing you'll get confused and stuck, and then find a coach. Having a professional coach (who actually coaches in emotional intelligence and transformation) can be instrumental. Sometimes it's just as effective to ask a friend to help you with this work! Get an emotional intelligence buddy and commit to helping each other see each other's shit!

It's *so* much easier to see someone else's shit, right? So open up to a trusted friend and get some prodding. It's invaluable. My clients say that the questions I ask during our coaching sessions can sometimes make their minds explode. Asking these questions accelerates their progress dramatically. You can have fast, frequent breakthroughs with the help of someone who does this work and is committed to your success.

Strategy 7: Protect Yourself from What Doesn't Give You Fuel and Energy

For this strategy, I want you to make different choices that are full of self-love. Some ways to do this include avoiding people who are energy vampires, avoiding numbing with excessive alcohol use or drugs, avoiding using distraction when you're faced with Key Moments (they are there to help you progress!), avoiding negativity of any kind, and please, please, please, avoiding judgement and shame. Don't engage in, or believe, any judgement or shame put upon you by others or that you direct at yourself. If they're judging you, it's about them and their issues.

I've seen from my own experience and the experiences of my friends and clients that this strategy can be really difficult. This is specifically because of our societal orientation toward duty and obligation. Remember the four main paradigms and how most people live in the paradigm of Duty? We've been programmed to believe that our function on this planet is one of meeting obligations and that we are valued for our grit, loyalty, and selflessness. We are constantly getting messages that we need to just shut up and do what needs to be done before we can do anything for ourselves. This is total matrix bullshit.

When I became a parent, I found myself feeling guilty when I took a little time to relax, have a nice dinner with friends, or simply play with my child instead of dealing with that stack of laundry. I had to start protecting myself from those toxic beliefs, as well as from people who were telling me what I "should" be doing with my time. I also had to start avoiding people who insisted on talking about things that drained my energy, like friends who want to spend hours complaining about their lives. I've had to give myself permission to pay attention to the things in life that drain me and create a boundary between myself and those things. I've also never been more grateful for any new habit I've adopted, and I encourage you to look at your own life to see where you might need to adopt new habits and beliefs.

Strategy 8: Celebrate Victories and Wins

The victories and growth that come with this work are, by nature, personal, silent victories. Remember, it's *your* path, and it's really difficult to share it in a way that someone can appreciate and celebrate with you. I've found that when I have these breakthroughs and express these revelations to a friend, they can't quite appreciate it for what it means to me. It's not their shit. They haven't had to jump this hurdle yet, or they did it so long ago they don't remember how hard it was.

It can be lonely. That's why it's so important to find ways to acknowledge your own progress and celebrate it! Find people who do appreciate your victories and share with them. Notice your joy and celebrate it. It's your North Star! Think of ways to treat yourself with happy experiences! Use joy and happiness as fuel for the work. Don't forget to notice the early wins and momentum. You are literally changing the world around you.

When we shift the way we interact with the world, it literally changes the physicality of the world around us. Various spiritual traditions and existential teachings have long-professed lessons about how our very presence and intention shape things around us. We don't fully understand it, but some would say that science is starting to uncover possible explanations for it. So do yourself a favor, get curious, and start to look for it. I and many other wiser, more studious people than me have found this to be true in our lives. We set intentions and visualize what we want in our lives, and that act alone starts to shift our days, experiences, and lives. Perhaps what's happening is that we are putting an intention out there and then just being more observant and noticing when those opportunities or gifts come our way. Either way, who cares?! When you start to think and feel differently and choose different actions, things start to show up differently in your life. Just go with it. It's crazy, and noticing it is so freaking fun!

Strategy 9: Feed Your Soul

This is a tricky one, y'all. I, along with *many* people, had some negative experiences in religion, and after a while, I felt I'd outgrown it and was actually deeply offended by some of the beliefs I'd been taught. They didn't serve me or my fellow humans, so I rejected religion as a whole. However, I'm also a pragmatist. I focus on what actually works. And what surprised the heck out of me on this journey of personal growth was that when I allowed myself to come back to spiritual, or existential, teachings, they helped me in very profound and tangible ways.

You don't have to accept anything that anyone tells you. Explore and create your own beliefs, with your North Star being what actually works to bring you joy, puts your life in harmony with those around you, and brings you fulfillment and peace. A lot of the concepts in this book can be found in spiritual teachings, existential ponderings, poetry, and religious teachings. Some are quite ancient, actually.

I've found that when we are seeking out truths about how to live our best lives—specifically about who we are and the nature of the universe and reality—we are unlocking the power to truly be who we are meant to be. I haven't found a person who's truly fulfilled who doesn't have some sort of belief system they have formed very intentionally.

What the beliefs are is less important than the actual exploration and learning you do. Like you, your beliefs will evolve and expand. Let me clarify. I'm not talking strictly about religion, though religion can absolutely be helpful in creating your belief system. When I say spirituality, I mean a search for existential truths, such as understanding the nature of life, the universe, and our place in it. What matters is that you grow in the awareness of your connection to something greater than you, be it God, the quantum field, source energy, chi, or whatever you resonate with. There shouldn't be any rules or dogma—just a quiet, peaceful inner connection to that higher vibration of source energy.

Being in nature might connect you to this, or maybe it's yoga, or exhilarating conversation, or meditation, or prayer. There's no wrong path, and there's no wrong connection. When it comes to spirituality and existential truths, we experience a lot of jadedness and judgement in our modern culture. That's all part of the matrix. I believe we are all connected to source energy and to one another, just like the extensive root systems of some species of trees that interconnect underground and form one gigantic organism.

How do I know this? I just feel it. I've allowed myself to study it and discuss it with others and then find my own sense of spirituality in my own way. Joy is my North Star. If something brings me more joy, I'll keep going on that path. Spending a little time on this spiritual path has fueled me and given me so much clarity and joy. And it can for you, too. Modern references to spirituality tend to refer to a subjective experience of a sacred dimension and the "deepest values and meanings by which people live," often in a context separate from organized religious institutions.

Many of us have baggage from past experience with various religions and belief systems, because humans have really gotten confused in this area. Believe me, I get it. Just step around the hype, the matrix, and the confusion around spirituality and find what works for you. Trust yourself. I know you'll do great! It's actually pretty freaking fun.

Finding meaning in a way that feels true and inspiring to you will save your life. Be curious. Try on different sizes or types of spiritual wardrobes. You'll eventually find resonance with what fuels you and bring you joy. Without meaning, we are rudderless and trapped in ego-driven, survivalist behaviors that do not bring us joy. So read, learn from others, and believe nothing until you find it to be true for yourself. Then, let it fan your flames for living a great life!

Strategy 10: Embrace Challenge

I was coaching an executive in the technology sector, and he often used techie terms to articulate his experiences. As he used the Adversity Cycle and started to see the benefits of it in his life, he exclaimed, "This tool is like a cheat code[2] for life! It's incredible! It's like a huge shortcut through the bullshit to get to the kinds of lessons and accomplishments that would have taken me years to realize!"

He's exactly right. With the right knowledge and tools, you don't have to wade through the darkness and confusion, slowly figuring things out. You can apply powerful, accelerating tools like the Adversity Cycle to cheat through the normal haze of slow progress, stress, and dissatisfaction. And do you know what the number one resource fueling this powerful cheat code is? *Challenge.* Ironically, challenge is the universe's biggest gift to help you progress on your path as a human, so you can live a life of joy, fulfillment, and peace. But the matrix has tricked you into thinking that any challenge, difficulty, or resistance that slows you down is *bad.* Don't fall for it. That's just your ego rearing its ugly head, and it's a total lie.

By doing this work and realizing the power of using my Key Moments and *all* adversity toward my own learning, I've begun to spring up with joy whenever I realize I'm facing adversity. I actually get excited. I put my Spidey Sense on high alert, and I tell the universe I'm watching and ready for the lessons. I'm exhilarated. Does this sound whackadoodle? It kinda is! It flies in the face of what the matrix and common culture want us to do.

This evolved naturally for me: The more I did this work and realized the value of it, the more invaluable teachings I received from my Key

---

2 Techopedia defines a cheat code as "a code, method or device used by gamers to advance levels, or to get other special powers and benefits in a video game."

Moments. And you know what? The same can happen for you. Progress and transformation really just mean leveling up. I've seen many clients start to overcome their Key Moments and learn beautiful, powerful lessons and think they are free from the grips of negative emotion completely. Months go by, and then WHAM! a full-on emotional tornado sweeps them up. That's the next lesson they are to learn. They come to me and say, "WTF? I thought I had progressed really far!" And I respond, "You *have!*"

When this happens it means you've leveled up, so this next lesson is for you up here, at the next level. You get to tackle a higher-level challenge for a higher level of learning. Isn't that great? And once you work through it and learn, guess what? There's another one coming. Embrace it. You have everything you need to learn from it, grow, and use it to reach new levels of joy.

Think of progression as driving a car with a standard transmission. You have to shift gears to get into the higher speeds, and there's a little deceleration, or sometimes even a choke, as you do this. It's the nature of momentum and progression. Face it: You're likely to choke up a little sometimes, especially when the difficulty level increases. Instead of getting upset or feeling defeated when this happens, celebrate it. It just means you're leveling up!

Aligning Yourself with the Universe

If you want to stay on the path of personal transformation, it must be a way of life, not something you think about occasionally. The Adversity Cycle is a cycle for a reason. It's meant to be used over and over, deepening your abilities, awareness, and skill in handling life in each of the four steps and their infinite applications. Each time you apply one of these steps to any circumstance that is challenging you, you will uncover deeper truths and more freedom from the matrix. The true point of this Adversity Cycle work is to align yourself with the way the universe actually works. It's being aware of how things actually work in the world around you and then knowing how to shift your beliefs and behavior to align with the way things work, resulting in a more joyful life.

The matrix is anything that distracts you from the truth about the way life works, or anything that tricks you into believing things that keep you out of alignment with the way things actually work! The more broadly and accurately you can apply the learnings along the way, the more components of your life will be improved. For example, I spent months just applying Step 3: putting my higher self in charge. I kept obsessing on this idea throughout my days: *What would my higher self do? What is truly important to me? What would it look like to live in this moment from that place?*

I realized that I was incredibly weak in this area. I hadn't explored it since I had turned away from religion in my twenties. I didn't realize I also had turned away from understanding what was truly important to me! Yikes! I started to build skill in quickly accessing my higher, or best, self and acting from it.

Each of these steps is actually a bundle of skills to develop. Using them in order, on a single Key Moment, is a vital start. Then, when you understand a particular step, take it and apply it wildly and creatively! There are no limits to the way you might want to apply it to build your skill. Then, when that next big Key Moment knocks you upside your head, your skills with each step will be more powerful—and frankly, you can move through it and learn what you're meant to learn *very* quickly and gracefully.

I see this book as the CliffsNotes on the greatest tools and skills to progress and level up as a fully alive human on this planet. Dive into any of these concepts much more deeply by doing more reading and talking with people. Avoid opinions and seek truth. Explore higher-level learnings. Your curiosity will take you exactly where you need to go. This book is a guide. Everything in this book can and should lead to more exploration. Follow your curiosity and see where it takes you!

Chapter 10

Reap the Rewards of Progression! The Ripple Effect of Joy

When I introduce the Adversity Cycle to my clients, I tell them it might be the hardest thing they've ever done. I tell them they are doing work that is so introspective and uncomfortable, it will likely push them to their limits. And then I ask them, "When you think back to the accomplishments that you are most proud of and the choices that have brought you the most fulfillment and joy, were they also the hardest?" Invariably the answer is yes. So here you are, at the end of the book, and hopefully neck-deep in some really hard, rewarding work. Congratulations! You're doing great! Now it's time to focus on the joyful, fulfilling benefits of this work, what I call the Ripple Effect.

The Ripple Effect

An executive I worked with noticed that she had a tendency to frequently use the thought distortion of personalizing during her Key Moments. Her reaction was to keep part of herself closed off to colleagues and never show any vulnerability. In our coaching work using the Adversity Cycle, she came to the realization that she wanted to stand up against her irrational fear of rejection or being perceived as an imposter, so she decided to be intentionally vulnerable with her three closest colleagues. After taking small risks with each of them, she came back to our session absolutely glowing. She exclaimed that she received back twenty times the rewards from her small gestures of vulnerability; her entire relationship with each of them felt fundamentally shifted and moving in a different, much more fulfilling direction. *That* is the Ripple Effect.

When we let go of our programmed, survivalist behaviors and begin to experiment with different choices while listening to our higher selves, the effect it has on the world around us is often far greater than anything we could have imagined. I get to hear these incredible success stories from clients over and over, and I experience them myself. Watch for the Ripple Effect from your new actions. Capture those wins by celebrating them, and say to yourself, "Yes, this! More of this!"

The Ripple Effect can be seen and experienced in two domains of life. The first domain is your internal experience, which includes your mental health, beliefs, state of being, joy, and the way you experience your daily situations and events. The second domain is your external experience, which includes everything in the world around you, such as your friends, family, colleagues, economic status, and home.

The Ripple Effect of this work creates changes in you and in the world around you. We'll start with the Ripple Effect in your inner domain and then move to its impact in your outer world.

Awareness

By far the most important element of the Ripple Effect is simply the transformation of your own inner experience and relationship with the world around you. I joke that since doing this work and breaking through a hell of a lot of the matrix lies, I might appear like someone who is mentally ill. I see the bullshit in all my thinking and laugh at it. I think I might actually know nothing and have very few opinions left to give. I believe that I can do anything and that I can literally shape the physical universe around me. I actually become excited when something "bad" happens in my life. I can honestly say I love everyone, even people who are hurting a lot of other humans on this planet. I see the potential of everyone and believe that most people are living in a different, clouded version of reality. They are asleep to the real universe and to real truth, but they believe they are wide awake.

Sounds crazy, right? Was it destabilizing and chaotic to do this work? Hell yes. It shook me to my foundation, and that is exactly what needed to happen to free me from all the lies. When you realize that almost everything you've believed is a lie, you feel crazy and scared. And then, as you start to call the matrix out on its bullshit, you start to realize how powerful you are, and you start to live from a place of power. You want to create a different world around you, because you actually know you can.

That's pretty freaking awesome! And it's right there, waiting for you. You're already growing in your ability to create and receive more joy. That is a whole new level of awareness. Coming up out of the hazy fog of confusion and lies, you start to realize the opportunity that each new day brings.

Freedom

The second Ripple Effect in your inner experience is the effect of becoming free—like really free. This is a *biggie*. Most people believe their negative thoughts and emotions, suffering costly mistakes and never realizing their dreams. Sadly, they believe *that* is the nature of existence. But we know better, right? That's the matrix.

But we have to experience a different internal reality to disprove those lies. And when we do that, we become freer from their grips on us every day. We can also be free from overpowering fear when we prove to ourselves that we can stand in the face of our fears and make choices that are scary, but better for us. In addition to disproving our own lies, we can free ourselves from other people's shit. That is, we can free ourselves from allowing other people's beliefs and behaviors to negatively affect us.

Remember, this work isn't intended to change the world *around* you. It's intended to change your experience of the world, so you can live a wiser, more intentional, joyful life that is free from suffering. However, I'll admit, when you make those integrity moves, it does change how people interact with you, and it changes the outcome of challenging situations, because you are navigating them much more effectively.

The work is really all about you. And, in the end, if we all do this work, the world can be transformed fundamentally by all of us together. When you free yourself from the matrix of lies, you can model that for others, and free them a bit as well. **Suffering is not necessary.** That freedom, my friends, is priceless.

Transformed Relationships

Now we're going to shift gears and talk about the Ripple Effect you are starting to create in the world around you as you work with the Adversity Cycle. This is actually the most common area where I see the Ripple Effect in the outer world, in my life, and in the lives of my clients. This really shouldn't be a surprise! If you have been even dabbling with the steps of the Adversity Cycle, I'd be willing to bet that you've already seen some changes in the quality of your relationships. I mean, most Key Moments involve other people, so if you are interacting differently with triggering situations involving other people, you're going to get different results, right? However, that is grossly underestimating the transformative power of the Ripple Effect! What I commonly see is illustrated in this example with one of my clients, Stuart.

Stuart is an incredibly intelligent physicist and successful entrepreneur. He was so focused on science and business, however, that he had understandably put a lot of his learning and attention into those areas and less on his own emotional intelligence or his relationships. Then—surprise, surprise—Key Moments started popping up on him left and right when it came to the relationships on his team.

Through our coaching work, he began to subtly shift the way he was approaching his leadership by interacting with conflicts differently, using moments of choice, processing the conflict or dysfunction through the lens of the Adversity Cycle, and then interacting with the situations from his higher self. He didn't think he was doing anything dramatically different, and no one had given him any feedback or reason to believe they perceived a big difference in his approach. Yet he was shocked at how differently he was interacting with his team and how differently they were interacting with one another.

It started with subtle differences, like people bringing coffee or treats for their team into the office and talking about what music they liked and playing different music as they worked. Then he noticed that people were sharing deep, personal things with him that they had never shared before. They were opening up and being more vulnerable, and they were collaborating *much* better with him and with one another. Their work started improving unexplainably, and the vibe in the office was vastly different than just a couple months prior.

When Stuart turned away from ego-based thinking, he influenced his team to subtly do the same. Together they transformed their work environment into a place that none of them had ever envisioned or hoped for, but now were so grateful for. Stuart told me he never even thought about whether or not he looked forward to coming into work, until now—when he realized he was excited to go to work for the first time in his life. The team still faced hardships and challenges, but they experienced those hardships very differently because they felt connected and united.

I've seen the Ripple Effect in marriages, families, extended families, and communities. I've seen one person using the Adversity Cycle to transform the way they were feeling about the people closest to them, and the Ripple Effect influenced their loved ones without their loved ones even doing this work. The beautiful reality of the Ripple Effect is that it's paying us back in ways that we hadn't even thought of or dared to dream. It is giving us far more benefit than we ever knew to ask for and far more than what should be expected from the amount of time and effort we put into it.

Social Empowerment

One of the most profound Ripple Effects of the Adversity Cycle in our lives is freedom from oppression and racism. Specifically, it's freedom from perpetuating oppression and racism and freedom from letting the oppressive views and actions of others dictate our decisions and take away our power. What if everyone were doing this work? What if we were all facing our fears and distortions and living lives of courage and love?

Have you ever heard someone say that fear is the root of racism? Or any *-ism*? It's natural (at least when you live in the matrix) to fear what is different—such as people who look or act differently from us and cultures that are different from our own. Fear is the root of distrust, because we think we won't be able to predict somebody else's actions, and we might be afraid they will hurt us.

Distrusting people, cultures, religions, and situations is the root of racism. It all boils down to self-preservation. And when we are on the receiving end of oppression, racism, or irrational distrust or marginalization of any kind, our fear is triggered. In these instances, fear causes us to sink into our ego-based beliefs that help us survive. It's natural and, at the same time, so unnatural, because it's all a lie. For example, when I believe I'm threatened, I think I have to prioritize my survival over my actions that are rooted in personal responsibility, purpose, and vision. I then perpetuate my own disempowerment, which in turn perpetuates the disempowerment of others.

Racism and the oppression of any group of people for any reason is rooted in fear and a lack of connection with our higher selves. The Adversity Cycle serves to empower us and move us out of the grips of fear and matrix in our lives, so we can reject the old habits and beliefs that hurt us and others. Remember, our ego often convinces us that we are powerless in Key Moments and that we must try to survive. But this doesn't allow us to do the work of Steps 2 and 3: finding the areas where we did have influence and either didn't use it or didn't use it well, and then making different choices based on our higher selves according to what is most important to us.

Racism, violence, and oppressive beliefs and behaviors are deeply rooted in ignorance and fear. This work, this book, is a weapon against the ignorance and fear in all of us. We all have the capacity to hurt others when we are living from a place of fear and old trauma. When we do this work on ourselves, we pull out of those old, dangerous patterns by uncovering our irrational fears, old trauma-based beliefs about the world that aren't rational or true, and approaches and ways of thinking that don't serve our lives. We begin to discover another way to live, one that defies those unhealthy patterns.

People aren't born racist; they aren't born abusers or oppressors. They got banged around by life, shaped their beliefs from a place of fear and pain, and now have gotten stuck living out those patterns. This work allows us to unlearn what we've come to believe as we've navigated fear, trauma, and even abuse in our own lives. As long as we keep merely surviving and pushing away reality and our Key Moments, we will continue to make irrational decisions like staying with abusive partners, choosing to be with people who hurt us, and continuing to think about the world in ways that hold us back.

As long as we operate in this survival program, we will continue to hurt others by acting out of fear and self-protection. We may hurt others due to our delusions and beliefs that are not grounded in reality, but rather grounded in fear and old trauma. We also protect ourselves by rejecting, blaming, and hating people we label as "bad" or "racist" or "violent." We protect ourselves by blaming and hating anyone we think is against us or what we care about, or anyone who has power over us.

We grow out of these behaviors of oppression, victimization, racism, hatred, superiority, and inferiority when we do the work of improving our emotional intelligence and using adversity to level up. It's our choice. And when we make the choice to get off the path of survival and get on the path of learning and creation, we become empowered. When this happens, we realize we don't have to live out that old crap anymore.

We actually have more choices and more influence than we have been letting ourselves believe. It's fully within our power to change ourselves. And it's also within our power to be a positive influence (not a control, but an influence) on others who are also suffering. But it's nearly impossible to be a positive influence on someone else when we are acting from a place of self-protection and fear. You can change yourself, and you can help others change. *That* is empowerment. And that is what this work is about.

A Black man at a company where I was conducting leadership coaching relayed this story. At the office one day, a white colleague said something that almost anyone would have considered a racist remark. Instead of walking away, pretending to ignore the offending remark, and resenting his coworker for hours or days, my client used his emotional intelligence tools.

This could have played out very differently and hurt both this man and his colleagues. For example, he could have stormed out, deciding the company tolerated racist comments or individuals and that he didn't want to work there any longer. He could have labeled his coworker as a racist. But that's the trick with labeling. We believe we can slap a judgement on someone's character. But do you feel it's accurate when someone slaps a label on you?

No one is as simple as a label. And because of that, no one is just a racist. We have been raised in a society with deeply embedded racism, and we can all work to move ourselves toward more awareness of the racist lessons we've learned. Labeling someone as a racist is a thought distortion and essentially an easy out. Placing the label does not acknowledge the complex truth about the situation: that we all have work to do when it comes to race and to ALL the *-isms*, and we all have the potential to help one another with that work. Labeling one another does no good.

I asked my client a simple question: "Who do you want to be when you are faced with a racist comment? Do you want to be someone who reacts and feels horrible, or do you want to be an agent of change? Because you can't do both. If you label him, become angry, and separate yourself from him, you cannot be an agent of change in his life. So, who do you want to be?"

My Black client, being his usual calm and thoughtful self, utilized his emotional intelligence toolbox, and, instead of labeling his colleague and walking away, he went back to his colleague and explained, "I regard what you said the other day to be really racist, and it offended me." The offending coworker thought a moment and acknowledged that it was probably a racist comment. My client had used the Adversity Cycle and avoided suffering—the suffering of an ignorant or likely unintended verbal blow. He put his emotions in check and took his power back.

Yes, we can be victims of a racist culture. But my client had a choice; he could label the offending white colleague and suffer pain from any further relationship issues or do what he did: plant the seeds for the white colleague to rethink his behavior, reexamine his beliefs, and try to understand why his Black colleague responded to him in a respectful and calm manner.

Did my Black client excuse the narrow behavior? No, he actually created an opportunity for change. He maintained his voice while providing a calm but clear opportunity for his white colleague to connect to their mutual humanity and forge a new relationship based on respect. This is a great example of connecting rather than labeling, of transforming rather than pigeonholing, and of empowering rather than disempowering.

Flow

You've already experienced this, but you probably think it's rare and fleeting. Flow is that state where you are so immersed in something, doing it for the sake of doing it, feeling so fulfilled, that you lose time. You could do it hours on end and be fully at peace. In the context of the Adversity Cycle, flow is often when you are truly living from the core of your higher self. You are being who you are meant to be, living in the moment, expressing your unique gifts, and unconcerned with silly things like survival, the past, or the future.

Yes, it's possible to flow through much of your waking hours instead of struggling and stressing or feeling anxious or overwhelmed. Flow is just experiencing the crazy world we live in, learning from the little challenges—and occasionally the big ones—without resentment, and knowing you can handle all of it.

Joy is your North Star, right? So, find what brings you joy by noticing what puts you in flow and give yourself more opportunity to do that! For many people, the path of creation allows them to flow while they are creating anything, be it a painting, a great dinner, a new relationship, or a new financial situation. I've been so devoted to this path that I'm now living in creation-mode almost all the time. Meaning, I'm looking at what I want and what I can create in my life, and I'm exhilarated to be in the process of making it happen. I'm loving the surprises and truly feeling like myself, doing what I was wired to do on this planet and seeing the beauty that this creates.

My most sincere wish for you, fellow human, is this: flow into joy. Figure out who you are, what you love, and then do it unapologetically.

The Ripple Effect of this work allows us to do just that: to uncover what brings us flow as well as what holds us back from experiencing flow. Watch how creative you are, see what you can build, and experience the Ripple Effect of fulfillment from what you do and feel when you are in flow!

Synchronicity

Synchronicity, as I use it here, is what some people in various cultures might call magic or luck. Whatever you want to call it, I can't deny the correlation of synchronicity and being on the path of learning and creation. I've seen this undeniably in my own life. When I spend more time on the path of survival, I don't have as much luck or things just going my way. When I am on the path of learning and creation, however, I receive an abundance of random gifts and support from others, along with chance interactions and encounters that bring me joy, clarity, ideas, or solutions to my challenges. The stars just align, and things come to me seemingly out of nowhere.

There have been a lot of different ancient teachings and ponderings about this factor, and many people have identified this phenomenon since the beginning of time. I'm not going to try to explain it to you with quantum physics, though this is a promising and interesting path to explore! In fact, I'm not going to try to explain it at all. It could simply be that when I'm not in survival mode and covering my ass, I see more opportunity and make different micro-choices that result in a ripple of different outcomes. It could be that I just notice great things coming to me more when I'm in creation mode and know what I want, and I might ignore those things when I'm not focused on what's important to me and building my life intentionally. I guess the explanation is just not that important to me. What is important to me is that I know beyond a measure of doubt that when I am spending a lot of my waking hours acting in accordance with my higher self, having vision and purpose in life, great luck and serendipity come my way in *huge* doses. For me, it's the most fun demonstration of the Ripple Effect of this work!

The Universe Has Your Back

I have to admit, when I started doing this work with clients, I used to say that you get back from this work what you put into it. If you don't use the tool and dig into the reflection and experiment with new behaviors, you won't see the benefits. While that is technically true, I've come to realize that the effort people put into the work of the Adversity Cycle is far outweighed by the benefits they receive. It's completely imbalanced—not even a close comparison.

I probably don't deserve the Ripple Effect of benefits to my life since I've been using the Adversity Cycle, but I'll happily take them all. I didn't believe that this level of awareness, freedom from suffering and oppression, and inspiration was possible—at least not for me. Trust that the universe has your back. The Ripple Effect is already happening for you. Look for it, pay attention to it, believe it, and, most importantly, be grateful for it. You've done the work. Now is the time to receive the reward.

AFTERWORD

A Moment in History: The Adversity Cycle During the COVID-19 Pandemic

I've been writing this book during an unprecedented time in the history of our world. While I was using the Adversity Cycle to help clients well before the COVID-19 pandemic and the corresponding social and political unrest, these weeks and months have truly shed light on the need for this tool and the need for personal introspection in general. I'm watching so many people hurt themselves, hurt others and put them at risk, and make terrible decisions for themselves and their families and communities. I've witnessed, as I'm sure you have as well, many people acting out of fear and ego, without having any awareness that they are doing so. Right now there are so many people acting in ways that are highly irrational while under the belief that they are absolutely on the right path, and anyone who disagrees with them is labeled wrong, bad, dangerous, and so on.

As I've been writing, studying, and using the Adversity Cycle with clients during this time of adversity, I've been able to have a more intense time of experimentation and reflection on the importance of staying on the path of transformation, learning, and creation as opposed to reverting to the path of survival. Survival mode is all around me at levels I've never before witnessed, and it's not pretty, y'all.

Following are some examples of the survival matrix path I have witnessed during this pandemic:

- I saw educated adults disbelieving there even was a pandemic or that COVID-19 was real, despite undeniable evidence to the contrary.

- Even after we had plenty of research showing how the virus was spreading and what activities were very low risk, I saw parents locking their children in the house, not allowing them to interact with any other children, and forcing them to scrub their hands every thirty minutes.

- Instead of taking care of their bodies, immune systems, and lungs, I saw people eating a lot of sugar and gaining weight. Others were using tobacco and drinking unhealthy amounts of alcohol. Often these same people complained about the risky behavior they perceived others engaging in while not taking basic steps to take care of themselves.

- I saw people bitterly, and sometimes violently, turning on their neighbors and friends in the wake of brutal police violence against people of color and the resulting protests.

- I saw people with serious health risks (such as needing to take immunosuppressants during cancer treatment) insist they were being incredibly cautious while simultaneously taking very irrational, unnecessary risks and then contracting the virus.

- I saw people refusing to take basic, easy measures like wearing a mask to help protect others and justifying it with an array of false beliefs.

Think about the examples in this list and how those choices may have been different if these people had the skills to see their thought distortions, to see how fear was driving their behavior, and to identify when their ego had run away with them. Imagine how different it would have been for those people if they had been able to take full responsibility for their health and the safety of their families and choose intentional approaches to navigate the risks of the pandemic. Imagine if these people took the time to connect with their higher values and principles, to identify what was really important to them, and to think about how they wanted to respond to the fear, violence, and sickness all around them. Imagine if these people had the skills to identify how fear was driving their behavior, to stop and identify what was really important to them, and then act in accordance with that. Imagine if we all looked for opportunities to live our best lives and be our best selves instead of being victims and blaming others. How would this pandemic experience be different for everyone if we were all looking for that win-win-win every day?

The clients I've been working with during the pandemic have said things like "If we hadn't started doing this work with you, we would have made some really horrible mistakes," and "We are so lucky to have been doing this personal development, because the challenges we faced were so new and troubling, I'm positive we would have been immeasurably more stressed and probably quite dysfunctional."

This last year has been a year of adversity at a whole new level, allowing me to see more clearly than ever the need for tools like the Adversity Cycle to help support people to make better choices for themselves and their lives. Personally, I've had a precious, wonderful year. I've kept this work at the center of my awareness and decision-making. Has it been hard? Yes, absolutely. Have I had moments of extreme frustration and sadness? Of course. But I've also spent so much time living from my higher self and being intentional about my days and who I want to be in the world. I've made the time to develop creative ways for my family to still have fun and be healthy. I've maintained faith in myself and those around me and not allowed the matrix to trick me into believing that I was being threatened when I was not.

The matrix has not been able to pull me into paranoia, and it hasn't been able to make me cavalier and irresponsible. I have used the adversity of this time to my benefit and have learned so many deep and profoundly helpful lessons about myself; I've learned more this year than any year of my life. The pandemic and quarantine are still in effect, with no clear end in sight, and I'm OK with it. I'm OK with whatever life brings me. I'll learn from it, and I'll be the best Meg I can be. And I'll continue to gain so much joy from the work I do, helping others live in this empowered, liberated, and loving way.

I don't resent the people I see making these irrational, often hurtful choices. I know that I have made all these same errors in judgement (and occasionally still do). They are no different from me. They have fear and egos and human brains, and they live in a matrix of lies, just like me. I've just pulled up out of the matrix with tools they don't have. I want that for them, just as I want that for you. I want you to be able to look back at crazy ass times like these and say, "I learned so much. I did great things. I lived a great life."

To me, the pandemic and the long stretch of quarantine have been a test of my emotional and spiritual skills. I'd often wonder: *How can I maintain empathy for all people during these trying times, regardless of how they put me or my family at risk of a serious virus? How can I be judicious and loving in my behavior every day, regardless of how drained and scared I might feel? How can I find a path of integrity in such troubling and chaotic times in our society? How can I let go of all the things that used to bring me happiness (parties, travel, adventure) and instead find solace in joy?*

The truth is I was able to do all of those things—not perfectly or 100 percent of the time, but I did them. I found empathy where I would have previously found hatred. I've been loving to people in situations that would have previously put me on the attack. I've let go of the things I was no longer able to do safely and shifted my focus intentionally. And guess what? I found plenty of joy—boundless joy when I looked for it and created it.

I engaged in joyful activities like a hike in nature with my son, frolicking around with my crazy puppy, discovering great restaurants for take-out food, cooking creatively, and finding fun new activities and games to break up the monotony. I am so proud (and a bit astounded) at how joyful this year of pandemic living has been for me. I'm proud, because I created it. All of it. And I'm astounded, because I know how I would have responded a few years ago before doing this work. I actually don't admit it to many people, because they don't understand, and their egos will flare up and accuse me of being selfish or delusional. (Yes, that has happened.) And quite honestly, part of the fuel for the fire that has driven me to write so carefully and so furiously over this last year has been watching the suffering of others and wanting to help. I want others to have the joy I experience. I want them to not get knocked down so easily by adversity and spiral into narratives of distortion and self-deception. I want this for you. It's not easy. But what highly rewarding experience in life has ever come easily?

ACKNOWLEDGMENTS

No author writes a book alone. I have so many people to thank for their support, wisdom, and encouragement as I meandered through this crazy process of book writing! First, my copilot in writing, Sandy Dochen—your wisdom and journalistic curiosity shaped this book profoundly. Thank you for keeping me going and almost keeping me on the straight and narrow. To my husband, Tommy, you really are my rock. I couldn't have done this without you picking up more than your fair share of the load at home and making me laugh at myself. To my incredible teammates at Mission Squared, thank you for your constant encouragement, your input, your critical feedback, and your deep engagement in this utterly insane path of personal transformation. I definitely couldn't have written this book and uncovered the real truths of what brings me joy without the teaching and disciplines from Dr. Morguelan. Thank you, Dr. B, for supporting me as I wrote this book and for allowing me to share my interpretations of these ancient teachings! And finally, to my higher self, thank you for finding me, guiding me, and pointing me down that path of life that will actually bring me joy—and, of course, for pretty much writing this book for me.

Appendix

People to Learn from as You Continue on the Path

As you continue to work with the Adversity Cycle, you will grow and evolve, and new curiosities may start to emerge. This work tends to bring up a lot of questions about the way our psychologies work, teachings about the way the world really works, and new perspectives about what it really means to wake up from the matrix. Because of this, I wanted to leave you with some resources to assist you as you start to level up and seek out new perspectives. I've grouped these resources by category to help you find what you're looking for more readily. While this is not a comprehensive list, it's a great starting place, and I hope you enjoy the materials listed.

I'm beyond proud of you and wish you every success as you rediscover your higher self and learn how to bring more joy and fulfillment into your life!

EMOTIONAL INTELLIGENCE
Daniel Goleman
Books: *Emotional Intelligence: 25th Anniversary Edition; Altered Traits; Science Reveals How Meditation Changes Your Mind, Brain, and Body; A Force for Good: The Dalai Lama's Vision for Our World*

Marc Brackett
Book: *Permission to Feel*
Podcast with Brené Brown: *Permission to Feel*

Dale Carnegie
Books: *How to Stop Worrying and Start Living; How to Win Friends and Influence People*

NEUROSCIENCE AND SOCIAL/BEHAVIORAL SCIENCE

Brené Brown
Books: *Daring Greatly; Dare to Lead; Rising Strong; Braving the Wilderness*
Netflix special: *The Call to Courage*

António R. Damásio
Books: *The Strange Order of Things; Self Comes to Mind*

Joe Dispenza
Books: *Breaking the Habit of Being Yourself; Becoming Supernatural*
YouTube videos and interviews
Podcast: *Joe Dispenza Audio Experience*

David Perlmutter
Books: *Brain Wash; Brain Maker; Power Up Your Brain: The Neuroscience of Enlightenment* (with coauthor Alberto Villoldo)

MODERN SPIRITUALITY AND EXISTENTIAL THOUGHT

Eckhart Tolle
Books: *The Power of Now: A Guide to Spiritual Enlightenment; A New Earth: Awakening to Your Life's Purpose*
Courses, events, and other resources: www.eckharttolle.com

Shinzen Young
Books: *The Science of Enlightenment: How Meditation Works; Beginner's*

Mind: Three Classic Meditation Practices Especially for Beginners coauthored with Jack Kornfeld and Sharon Salzberg

Deepak Chopra
Book: *Total Meditation: Practices in Living the Awakened Life*
Resources: www.deepackchopra.com

Cindy Wigglesworth
Book: *SQ21: The Twenty-One Skills of Spiritual Intelligence*

Jed McKenna
Book: *Spiritual Enlightenment: the Damnedest Thing* (The Enlightenment Trilogy Book 1)

Margaret Wheatley
Book: *Who Do We Choose to Be? Facing Reality, Claiming Leadership, Restoring Sanity*
Books, classes, and resources: www.margaretwheatley.com

Vishen Lakhiani
Book: *The Buddha and the Badass: The Secret Spiritual Art of Succeeding at Work*

Dr. Barry Morquelan
Founder of Energy for Success. Dr. Morquelan is a master of a five thousand-year-old system from China, using source energy to wake up, be energized for life's adversities, and incorporate a structured, ancient system to overcome the matrix and bring more source energy into all aspects of your life.
To learn more: www.energyforsuccess.org

About the Author

Meg *is a grateful mom, daughter, sister, wife, and friend.* She grew up in Bloomington, Illinois, and attended Goshen College, a Mennonite College in Indiana. Meg then ventured out of the Midwest and eventually landed in Austin, Texas, first to study in the master's program at the University of Texas at Austin's School of Social Work, and then to pursue her career in service to others.

Meg's greatest joys are her small family, a wide array of sports, conversation of all kinds, sparking growth and joy in others, meditation, reading, and helping leaders pull out of the matrix to achieve new levels of success. In 2017, Meg launched Mission Squared, an organizational development firm committed to "transforming organizations by transforming their people."

Meg is a visionary and a proven leader in both local and national arenas. She is passionate about empowering other leaders to drive change, get better results, and solve organizations' most complex problems. Meg integrates her personal success as an executive with her passion and talent for transforming other leaders to achieve a track record of successful executive clients and organizational leaders in nonprofit, government, and for-profit sectors.

Meg loves sparking transformation and inspiring other change agents through her work with clients, her writing, and her speaking engagements at conferences and gatherings of leaders. While she still experiences the matrix in her own life, she now sees matrix experiences as an opportunity to leap to the next level of joy awaiting her.

CPSIA information can be obtained
at www.ICGtesting.com
Printed in the USA
BVHW081704110123
656096BV00019B/161